T0287037

ROVERS TILL I DIE

ROVERS TILL I DIE

The Story of Bob Crompton,
Blackburn's Most Famous Son

Harry Berry

First published by Pitch Publishing, 2023

Pitch Publishing
9 Donnington Park,
85 Birdham Road,
Chichester,
West Sussex,
PO20 7AJ
www.pitchpublishing.co.uk
info@pitchpublishing.co.uk

© 2023, Harry Berry

Every effort has been made to trace the copyright.
Any oversight will be rectified in future editions at the
earliest opportunity by the publisher.

All rights reserved. No part of this book may be reproduced,
sold or utilised in any form or transmitted in any form or by
any means, electronic or mechanical, including photocopying,
recording or by any information storage and retrieval system,
without prior permission in writing from the Publisher.

A CIP catalogue record is available for this book
from the British Library.

ISBN 978 1 80150 379 2

Typesetting and origination by Pitch Publishing

Printed and bound in Great Britain by TJ Books Limited, Padstow, Cornwall

Contents

Dedicated to my son Karl,
and grandsons Archie,
Izaak and Arlo.

A thank you to my friend Jim
Wilkinson for persuading me
that I should contact Pitch with
my manuscript.

Introduction

IT IS almost certain that there is no one alive who saw Bob Crompton play. There are probably several of us who knew someone who did see the great man in action, although whether we can still accurately recall conversations about him is a moot point. Speaking personally, those who had seen Crompton were my grandmother's brothers, Walter and Harry Haynes. Maybe time has played tricks with my memory, but I always thought that they had ambivalent feelings about the man. They never questioned his footballing greatness, nor doubted that he towered over not just football at the Rovers but the whole of England. Yet there was a strange lack of warmth about their recollections, devoid of humorous anecdotes and with only vestiges of the pride I expected for a local boy who had conquered the world. It was discordant with the stories I read in my childhood football annuals, where Crompton was regarded as a deity. After nearly 70 years of following the Rovers, I decided to try and seek explanation and discover the story of Blackburn's greatest son.

Broad-limbed Bob, a captain bold,

Renowned the wide world over,

The Rover who from Blackburn's fold,

Has never been a Rover.

'*The Buff*, 1915'

1

Beginnings

THE DAY of 26 September 1879 was a not untypical autumn day in Blackburn. South-west winds buffeted Lancashire, often becoming squally with outbreaks of rain. There was nothing propitious in the day to suggest the imminent arrival of someone who was to become Blackburn's most famous citizen. At 1 Harwood Street, a mile from the town centre, Alice Crompton delivered a strong, sturdy youngster, her third son, who was named after his father, Robert. He was to become England's greatest footballer, captain of his country and a legend of the game, the definitive full-back recognised by unanimous acclaim. Oddly, he was not to be the first man living in Harwood Street to play for his country, nor indeed the first full-back.

Harwood Street is located north of Blackburn Town Hall. It links Furthergate to Stanley Street and is in the district known as Little Harwood. It was not until 1856 that the council allocated the money to lay sets on the street and, even then, there were objections that the traffic did not justify such expenditure. There was nothing exceptional about Harwood Street. It was like many Lancashire streets of the time. There were few men unemployed and, although most worked in the cotton industry, there were engineers, bookkeepers, clerks and a police constable (William Nuttall), among the others. At number 31 was William Edward Lee, three years older than Crompton and destined for the mills, but a man who was to be a playing colleague of Crompton at Blackburn Trinity. There was an ample provision of the usual shops (grocer, baker, newsagent) but a strange preponderance of licensed victuallers (including Crompton's father), one such establishment for every shop, which requires some explanation. The street of some 125 residences had the following active beer sellers: Robert Crompton (1), Joseph Edwards (3), George Strong (12–14), James Thompson (17–19), Richard Dunn (71) and Lawrence Moulden (141).

The town had the highest proportion of liquor licences to dwelling houses in the country, one for every 34 houses. It was a consequence of being at the hub of the industrial revolution. At one time 40 per cent of the country's cotton exports came from the looms in Blackburn. Housing was poor and insanitary. A quarter of the children born did not reach their fifth birthday. Working hours were long, dangerous, and tedious. Alcohol was widely available and was used by the men as an antidote to their harsh lives. When there is a demand, there is usually a supplier, and many Blackburn men seized the chance to avoid the mills and become more prosperous.

A few continued their upward momentum. William Greenwood had started his family on the route to financial security when he owned the White Bull at Salford Bridge. His son Richard had the foresight to see that selling liquor was a competitive business and might ultimately have its limits. He moved into the cotton trade and soon had a mill employing 280 people. He had five sons, William, Richard, Thomas, Henry and Doctor, all of whom were able to enjoy the good life so much that they were able to attend Windermere College or Malvern College and retire at an early age. Three of the five played for Blackburn Rovers and Doc Greenwood preceded Crompton in the England right-back shirt.

Of course, location was everything and an inn in Little Harwood was never going to be as remunerative as one at Salford Bridge in the centre of the town. Away from the town centre, licensees needed to be resourceful. Fate gifted the elder Crompton an unusual opportunity. Close to his premises was a pond which resulted from mining activities. Four men were killed in December 1819 in an underground explosion and a row of cottages nearby became known as 'Blow Up Cottages', as a grisly reminder. The pond was acquired by a group of Scottish expatriates who turned it into a curling rink.

Blackburn had acquired a large Scottish population. At the vanguard of the Caledonian influx were the Scottish drapers. From the start of the 19th century Scots came from the Border towns such as Annan, Dumfries and Wigtown, and settled in Blackburn. They traded in drapery and tea and sold door to door, on weekly credit. The town was convenient for them to cover the whole of north Lancashire and they spent most of their working lives on the road. So great were their numbers that in 1837 they formed the Blackburn Scottish Travellers' Association for the Better Protection of the Trade. Their chief aim was to reduce the bad debts they occurred by means of sharing information about their customers. Many of them became pillars of Blackburn society, the best-known being John Rutherford.

Rutherford was born in the town, the son of an itinerant draper from Rigg, near Gretna, who had entered into partnership with Henry Shaw in the Salford Breweries. Beer made the family rich. After starting his education at Lower Bank Academy in Dukes Brow, Rutherford moved on to Annan Academy (where his father had the family estate), Lancaster Grammar School and Glasgow University. He returned to Blackburn, but his father died in 1878 and Rutherford took over as manager at the brewery. He was to be elected mayor of the town in 1888, served for 27 years in parliament as MP for Darwen, during which he won six elections, and was subsequently knighted. He also won the St Leger in 1925 with his horse Solario. Despite his estate in Scotland, he kept house in Blackburn, constructing the Beardwood Mansion off Preston New Road.

William Thom was the son of a draper from Annan. He was born in John Street in 1842, where most residents were Scots, and went on to form the engineering company Foster, Yates and Thom which supplied mill engines and steam boilers to the developing world.

The Jardine brothers, William and John, came from Annan and established their drapery business on Ainsworth Street. William's son, Joseph, worked as an agent but is best remembered for being the most prominent member of the Blackburn poets' movement. It was John who introduced curling to the town, forming the Blackburn Caledonian Society, which played at Audley. They contested games against teams from Preston and Southport, but fixtures were limited by the weather and depended on freezing conditions on Saturdays. In those days, winters were harder so games were not uncommon, but it helped to have opposition in town and as a consequence the Rose and Thistle Curling team was formed, although most of the members held dual membership with the Caledonian Curling Club. John Rutherford, who was to prove a benefactor to Crompton later, became president of the Rose and Thistle team.

At their best, Rose and Thistle's hopes of winning both the Lancashire and FA Cup, expressed at their general meeting, were not met with disbelief. In April 1886 they came third in the Holden Challenge Cup at the Southport Glaciarium, beating Shettleston 17-11, Blackburn Caledonians 15-14 and Liverpool 24-14. John Jardine's son, also John, qualified as a solicitor, was captain of the town's rugby union side and later moved back to Annan to take up the post of Provost.

Other Scottish draper families were the Geddes and Wells clans from John Street, the Hyslops from Inkerman Street, the McKies from Victoria Street, and the Bells from Brook Street. An occasional player was the famous Rovers defender Hugh McIntyre. Although the participants were predominately Scottish there was the odd English player. The Yorkshire-born landlord of the Waterloo Hotel in Penny Street, Francis Prest, was one of the most skilled exponents of the game.

The Cromptons' inn, in Greenbank, had been named the Rose and Thistle Inn by Rutherford, whose company Henry Shaw & Co. owned it. It was christened in deference to his origins in two countries. Having the owner of the brewery frequently attend his hostelry socially helped Crompton in his struggle for survival against the glut

15

of beer houses in town. Rutherford took him under his wing and when his company acquired the grocer's shop at 143–145 Harwood Street, which had been run by Robert Lupton, and turned it into an inn, Crompton became the tenant. Transferred with him was the name of his previous inn. Henry Shaw & Co. was a rival to the other brewery chains, Thwaites, Duttons and Nuttalls. It owned many inns in town, among them the Sun Inn, Astley Gate, Nelson Inn, Park Road, Gardener's Arms Inn, Great Bolton Street, Montague Arms, King Street and General Wolfe Inn, Northgate.

Curling was not the only sport that had adherents at the Rose and Thistle. They also had a football team. Historically in Blackburn they played cricket in the summer varied with occasional athletic sports but just before Crompton's birth a new game called association football, which was developing through a variant of rugby called Harrow rules, had started. In 1872 a club was established in the nearby village of Turton but in town there were only a handful of games, almost all at the instigation of a man called Albert Hornby. The Hornbys had played a huge part in the development of the town. It was Albert's grandfather John who started the dynasty, entering the cotton trade with such effect that he was able to build himself a mansion on King Street. His son William Henry (born 1805) was to further the empire. A marriage to the sole heiress of Edward Birley of Kirkham helped enhance the family prospects and his business interests prospered to the point where his mills employed 1,400 people, with Brookhouse Mill his largest. In addition, he entered politics, became chairman of the Blackburn Conservative Party at the age of 27, the town's first mayor in 1851 and with sufficient children (11) to look after the business was elected as one of the town's two MPs, serving from 1857 to 1867.

Albert was sent to Malvern College where he excelled in all sports, being so small and agile when he took up cricket that they nicknamed him 'Monkey', which remained with him all his life. Around the time that Turton was forming a football club, Albert was working in his father's mills, being groomed for a managerial role. Ever keen to indulge in sport he encouraged the workers to kick a ball around in their brief breaks or after work.

It was a brave move for the son of the boss to play with the weavers and tacklers. Conditions in the mill were hard and there were many who held grudges against the owner. Hornby proved that he could match the toughest, was totally unafraid and won a grudging acceptance from the workers. His father had possessed the same ability to command respect. In 1835, following the parliamentary election in which the Conservative candidate defeated the reform candidate, he had taken a celebratory drink at the Bay Horse and on leaving was passing over Salford Bridge when a mob spied him and decided to avenge their defeat. They threw him over the parapet so that he landed in the mud on the east side. Rescued by some of the Conservative faithful he laughed off the assault, asking his helpers merely for an escort to the local hatters to replace the one which had floated off downstream. When Albert Hornby asked the mill workers to form a football team they agreed. Hornby undertook to provide the opposition.

He recruited these from his circle of friends. His brother Harry, who later followed his father into parliament and was subsequently knighted, was ever keen for a sporting challenge. Whenever the town staged a sports day the names of Albert and Harry were always on the entry sheet. Naturally enough Harry played for Albert's team. So did Arthur Appleby, son of an Enfield mill owner and subsequently a Lancashire cricketer, and Joseph Law, the town's bookseller who subsequently set up business in London. There were also John Pickering, the shuttle maker, and John Baynes, the first person to enrol at the reopened Blackburn Grammar School, who became a man of the cloth. The Hornbys called their team the 'Rovers' and they took part in several encounters with the workers from the Hornby mills. Their most difficult opponents were the Brookhouse team, captained by Albert. A team of the time contained William Hill (blacksmith), William Graham (labourer), William Leeming (weaver), Stephen Fawcett, Ralph Duxbury (spinner), William Little (spinner), John Farren, Thurston Hesketh (foreman), Henry Cottam (weaver) and John Eastham (weaver).

Later the games ceased as Albert moved on. He started to live in Cheshire and the development of football in east Lancashire passed to Darwen, who were situated just over the moor from Turton. The initiative to form the Lancashire FA came from Darwen, in 1878, and within the next few years football clubs shot up all over east Lancashire, particularly in Blackburn. Teams were formed by members of existing cricket clubs, churches, public houses or simply from groups of streets. Interest around the Rose and Thistle was so great that they were able to run a reserve team. A field was secured, at nearby Whitebirk, for their games and by 1881 their results were reported in the local press. Sam Bleasdale, a weaver from Charlotte Street, led the attack. It is impossible to know how good they were but on 3 December 1881 they beat Excelsior 10-0. It is not known if Robert Crompton senior took part in games but as he had turned 30 it is doubtful if he would have done so. Indeed, it is known that he was opposed to his son taking up the game and once burnt his boots so that he could not play. The team remained in existence until about 1895, playing in the Blackburn League which became the North-East Lancashire League. By then young Robert had commenced to appear for them.

The young Robert attended Moss Street School. It was located just up the road from Harwood Street, in Clinton Street. Not being a free school, parents had either to pay themselves or apply to the board of guardians for their fees to be met. In 1891 the membership of the school was 174 boys, 134 girls and 307 infants. By virtue of the fact that it was not a free school, there were always vacancies and at the time it had 81. St Stephen's, situated less than 200 yards away, had 186 vacancies. When Crompton was a schoolboy there was little organised school football in town. It was not until 1897 that local schoolmasters started to organise interschool competition, for a cup provided by a local entrepreneur, Harry Boyle.

In June 1891 there was a significant appointment that altered the emphasis of the school to the sport, although it was too late to affect Crompton, who had moved on to the Parish Higher Grade School. A local man, Henry Ashton, was appointed headmaster at a salary of £150 per year. A champion of all sports, he encouraged football and athletics and became chairman of several local bodies connected with sport in schools. At the time of his application for the job he was teaching in Brafferton in Yorkshire but had commenced as a pupil teacher at St Thomas's North School. When he was 17, in 1879, he had started playing at left-half for Rovers' reserves but his time at the club was cut short when he went to teacher training college at Culham in Oxfordshire. He was one of several pupil teachers (Dilworth Hartley and William Waring were others) who the Rovers signed at a time when they had to make the transition from being a club for the sons of mill owners and successful tradesmen, to operating on more democratic lines. They had no desire to incorporate the working men from the Blackburn mills into the team and sought to bring in the pupil teachers, trainee solicitors, accountants and bank employees as a means of avoiding turning the club into an egalitarian society. At the Higher Grade School Crompton played in the school football team alongside a boy named John Sweeting. Sweeting started work as a clerk at the Salford New Brewery, owned by Henry Shaw & Co., in 1894 and retired in 1939, as the assistant manager of Daniel Thwaites & Co., which had merged with Henry Shaw during this time. He also became a referee in the Lancashire Combination.

Crompton had already been subject to proximity with a footballing influence. At number 21, ten doors down from the house where he was born, lived the Ward family. Joe Ward, his wife Ellen and his four children (John Robert, Jane, James Henry, and Ellen) were all weavers in the cotton mills. They were a boisterous family who lived life to the full, particularly Jim Ward, who was a robust, athletic young man. The family were accustomed to spending time in the ale houses, eating well and gambling, which were the pleasures of the period for working-class Blackburnians. In young Jim they had the perfect vehicle for wagers. He could run as fast as anyone in town (he beat a local pedestrian Chippendale for a substantial bet), once leapt the nearby Leeds and Liverpool Canal (another bet in a contest with a local jumper, Aulty) and was a champion at a game, almost unknown elsewhere, called buck, as the following report from the *Blackburn Standard* of 10 April 1886 indicates:

'A great buck match for £30 took place between James H. Ward of Blackburn and John Catlow of Wilpshire, in a field at Whitebirk on Saturday afternoon. Great interest was taken in the event which attracted between 500 and 600 persons. Both men are well-known players, but they have never met before. The match, which was a single-handed one, was played with 4in bucks and round-headed sticks. Each player had 21 rises and during the progress of the match considerable betting was made. Ward was decidedly the favourite and 6-4 was freely laid on him. On the first rise Catlow took the lead but Ward immediately overtook him and finally won easily by 230 yards. The scoring was Ward 2,400 and Catlow 2,170 yards. The best hit made by each player was 140 yards.'

The game was played in Blackburn between 1850 and 1900 and was also known as 'tip cat' or 'guinea pig'. It was a dangerous game and countless locals were prosecuted for playing it in the streets. Basically, the game consisted of hitting a buck with a 2ft-long stick. The stakes depended on the quality of the players but for men like Ward (who defeated the previous champion, Smalley) the money was high and the associated gambling huge.

It was on the football field that Ward was best known. Football supremacy in the town had polarised into a straight contest between Blackburn Rovers and Blackburn Olympic. The differences between the clubs were not just sporting but social. Rovers had been founded by the sons of the town's mill owners and they had ensured that their members only came from the upper social circles. As a consequence, the working-class players gravitated to Olympic, formed from the amalgamation of two of the ad hoc clubs who had mushroomed in the town, Black Star and James Street.

Blackburn had in the previous 50 years been transformed by the invention of the loom. Factories had sprung up everywhere and a handful of men with initial resources and acumen had become enormously rich. Most were local men who had taken their newfound wealth and built or bought huge mansions on the edge of the town. They flaunted their wealth and dabbled in politics to ensure that the status quo was preserved. Their sons did not even work like their fathers and often retired at an early age having done little work. In 1901 Doc Greenwood, one of the early Rovers, did not even used the standard 'living on own means' to describe his occupation in the Census but without a hint of irony merely described himself as gentleman. In a short period of time Blackburn had seen more people become millionaires than any town in the country. Their money was made at the expense of the workforce, who lived in insanitary conditions, worked long hours in an injurious environment and received bare minimum wages. Life expectancy was poor, infant mortality appalling and the continuity of employment hazardous as the ebb and flow of the cotton industry frequently resulted in workers being laid off.

In 1842 and 1878 the labour force had rebelled. Sparking the first was the general election of 1841 when two Tory mill owners, William Fielden and Harry Hornby, were opposed by the Whig, William Turner, for the two seats available. The most popular of the trio was Turner but his support was strongest among people who had no vote, being disenfranchised because of lack of means. Unrest was in the air. The Corn Laws kept the price of corn artificially high by limiting foreign imports. The Chartists were agitating for one man, one vote but were being rebuffed by parliament, which wished to limit democracy to men of means. When Turner lost by a single vote, rioting broke out and was swiftly put down. A year later discontent still simmered. Chartists were surging through towns, stopping factories and halting production. In August a group of them arrived in Blackburn from Accrington, closing mills and having their numbers swelled by the workers. In Blackburn, the magistrate John Fowden-Hindle gathered his forces, the police under Superintendent Sheppard and a detachment of 72nd Highlanders under Colonel Arbuthnot. By the time the mob arrived in Darwen Street, having closed the mills en route by pulling the plug that let the steam from the boilers, the authorities were waiting and some of the ringleaders were arrested. As they were being loaded into a coach to take them to Preston an effort was made to release them. In the chaos that followed the order was given to fire and several were wounded. Within days the mills were back to full production, the ringleaders imprisoned and the workers had lost.

The workers were subdued until 1878 when after years of restricted working a cut of ten per cent in workers' wages was enforced. This was agreed by the Cotton Masters Association, whose chairman was a Blackburn mill owner named Robert Raynsford Jackson. In a summer of sporadic skirmishes mills were vandalised but the Cotton Masters ignored them. In desperation a mob descended on Jackson's house in Salesbury, looted it and burnt it to the ground.

Again, the action achieved nothing. The ringleaders were jailed, and the pay decreases stood.

This history of working-class struggle explains how Rovers and Olympic were so polarised. By the time Rovers realised that their reliance on the sons of the wealthy might be self-defeating, the die had been cast. Initially Rovers were superior because their players had been better nourished from childhood, were taller, stronger and could make their physical superiority count. This was countered by the superior ability of the working men, who actually tried to improve their skills in contrast to the gentlemen who never accepted the disciplines of regular training and would often not turn up in inclement weather.

In 1882 Rovers had reached the final of the FA Cup, where they lost to Old Etonians. Hoping to strengthen the side they utilised their greatest asset, the wealth of the members, and sought to undermine the Olympic by enticing their players with financial rewards. They had previously managed to lure the winger John Duckworth, but the rest of the Olympic players remained true to their class allegiances and turned down the greater rewards offered them until the little full-back, Joe Beverley, succumbed to the magic of cup dreams and defected to Rovers. The defection of Beverley had symbolic meaning to the working men who supported the Olympic. Yet Beverley, although born and bred in Blackburn, had little understanding of the depth of feeling. His father was a Chelsea pensioner, originally from Derbyshire, who had served all over the world. His mother, a Dorset midwife had trained in Dublin. His elder brothers were born in Newfoundland and Chatham. However, the man who was the alpha male in the dressing pavilion was Tommy

Gibson. Beverley had crossed the line in the sand when he joined the Rovers, but Gibson, whose services were coveted by the Rovers, treated their offers with disdain and the players to a man followed his lead.

Beverley's replacement was Jim Ward who was at the time only 17 but knew all about local working-class solidarity. He settled into the side alongside Squire Warbuton and brought a zest and athleticism that actually improved the Olympic side. Under the direction of the veteran English international Jack Hunter, who had fled from Sheffield football amid charges of professionalism, Olympic reached the FA Cup Final. The previous year, Rovers had been taken aback by the force and vigour of Old Etonians and for a time Olympic almost succumbed. That they did not was due to the directions of Hunter, who found in his hour of need that no one responded better than Ward, who could match the Etonians for vigour and had a fire in his belly. Ultimately Olympic rallied, won the game and became the first provincial winners of the FA Cup.

In March 1885 Ward became the first Olympian to play for his country. In Little Harwood his participation was the subject of long celebrations. If Crompton had a role model in sport, Ward did not provide a role model in life. Olympic assisted him in obtaining the tenancy of the Prince of Wales in Furthergate but the larger clubs were sniffing around. Accrington offered him a piano for the snug if he would transfer to them and Ward accepted, only to be intercepted by his father and brother who marched him back to the Hole i'th Wall ground of Olympic. In 1886 he finally left Olympic for Rovers, but he was never happy in a blue-and-white shirt and left the club. He had married and had a young son but neither his marriage nor his business survived, and he moved to Brierfield, where he worked in the Duxbury Arms. His attitude to the game was at best tenuous. *Athletic News* censured him for smoking while keeping goal and his career ended in December 1889 in unusual circumstances. A great trencherman, he indulged heavily with both knife and fork and tankard, made one wager too many (that he could clear a bar room table), failed and injured himself so badly that he never played again. He died young and forgotten before the turn of the century.

Apart from the close presence of Ward, Crompton grew up in a small town immersed in football. The success of Olympic in the FA Cup was immediately followed by three consecutive FA Cup wins by Rovers, which meant that for four years Blackburn was the home of the trophy. In addition, a succession of Blackburn men represented England. Doc Greenwood, the Hargreaves brothers, Jim Forrest, Jim Brown, Joe Lofthouse, Herby Arthur, Nat Walton, Jack Yates, Edgar Chadwick, Bill Townley made for a dazzling array of talent, all of whom could be encountered on the local streets. There can have been few local lads who were not inspired, and the local Sunday School football leagues were competitive breeding grounds for blossoming talent.

Despite his liking for the game, Crompton made no rapid progress. Part of the reason was that he was probably a more talented swimmer than a footballer and spent more time in the water than kicking a ball. He learned to swim at the Corporation Baths in Freckleton Street, where the superintendent was a namesake, George Crompton. Born in Wiltshire, George Crompton had once had a cotton manufacturing business in Lune Street. Once prosperous, it became a victim of the economic climate and in March 1878 he filed for bankruptcy, owing £1,700 and having assets of only £600. Edward Rushton was appointed as receiver for the business and Crompton and his wife were among 59 applicants for the posts of superintendent and matron of the public baths and wash houses a few months later. In July four were shortlisted with the recommendation that the post be given to Crompton who clearly had friends among the businessmen who ran affairs in the town.

Bob Crompton is first recorded in swimming competition at the Blackburn Gala of 1895 when he finished third in the 60 yards behind J.W. Coe (Osborne) and H. Gillow (Accrington). In the Blackburn Gala of 1898, Crompton was the most handicapped of the Blackburn entrants, with a handicap of nine yards. He won through to the final where he finished third, behind Walter Chadwick, one of the four footballing Chadwick brothers who included another English football international, Edgar. Chadwick had three yards' advantage over Crompton on the handicap, but the pair were beaten by W. Platts of Bolton.

It was, however, as a water polo player that Crompton made the most impact. The *Lancashire Daily Post* of 9 September 1898, reporting on a game between Blackburn and Darwen, stated, 'Blackburn played as seldom before and won by seven goals to two. The best man in the water was R. Crompton, the Blackburn half-back, who excelled himself. His shooting for goal was most accurate and his defensive work of the most determined description.' The Blackburn water polo team of the time was: J. Morgan/J. Bell (goalkeeper), J. Atkinson and J.G .Kay (backs), Crompton/J. Robertson (half-back), J. Redfern, H. Ward/F. Jones, G. Brown (forwards). Proof that Crompton was something of a local celebrity can be gathered by the fact that only he ever had his Christian name included in reports.

The other star of the team was Joe Kay, a hairdresser from Fielden Street who ran the swimming club. At the turn of the century he was appointed swimming instructor to Blackburn Corporation. In 1906 his views on mixed bathing were solicited and his opinion that he thought it could be advantageous caused local controversy. Alderman Law objected, claiming, 'It would lower the morals of our boys and girls.' Kay's female counterpart at the Corporation, Miss Hodgson, stated, 'Not for Blackburn. It would never do.' Bishop Thornton refused to believe that mixed bathing was immoral but thought for practical reasons it would be inexpedient. The Rev J.P. Wilson, president of the Free Church Council, 'failed to see that anything would be gained by it'. Support came only from an unexpected source. Mrs Lewis, the temperance advocate and sister of Rovers founder, John Lewis, stated, 'At first sight the proposal had a repugnant appearance to me, but I must frankly confess that when the subject is examined, we can hardly find much objection to it.'

Kay's nephew, Harry, became a champion long-distance swimmer who in 1906 beat the well-known American Carl Michelsen over five miles of the Acushnet River. George Brown, a utility player who later took Crompton's place at half-back, became the first Blackburn water polo player to play for Lancashire, when he played against Western Counties in 1904. The same year he came sixth in the Mersey mile. He joined Blackburn Swimming Club in 1892 and played with the water polo team until 1906, when he accepted the position of swimming instructor at the newly built Belper Street baths. In doing so he forfeited his amateur status and was lost to the game.

2

Football enters the life of Bob Crompton

THERE WERE several Cromptons in Darwen when sport started to multiply around 1880. Written records of cricket, football and athletics in the town are extensive but only one man of the name is recorded as a participant. John Crompton, a right-half, played for Darwen and later Old Wanderers. He played for Darwen Rovers in the first Lancashire Junior Cup Final, in 1886. He was not an immediate relative of Bob Crompton, who played his first organised football with the Rose and Thistle team in the North-East Lancashire League Second Division. By that time the team was on its last legs, affording the *Blackburn Times* to have some fun. In February 1895 the newspaper wrote, 'The Rose and Thistle managed to retain their good name. They cling to the wooden spoon like ivy to a wall except that the ivy climbs up the wall whilst they never climb the league ladder.' A month later it added, 'Rose and Thistle's intention is to take the wooden spoon to the annual dinner and there make good use of it.'

The only action in the close-season of 1895 was to wind up the club and withdraw from the league. Crompton had no difficulty finding a new club, initially moving to St Peter's in the Sunday league before quickly making the logical decision to move to Blackburn Trinity, who also played at Whitebirk. The club had started in the early days of Blackburn football in 1879 under the name of the church, Holy Trinity. They played not only in the North-East Lancashire League but also in the Blackburn Sunday School League, which increased Crompton's sporting commitment. When the Trinity played St John's in the Sunday School League at Hole i'th Wall on 28 September 1895, they lined up with: J. Miller, R. Crompton, W. Taylorson, T. Miller, W. Norris, W. Lee, A. King, J. Dewhurst, F. Wilkinson, J.W. Greenhalgh and E. Brindle. Most of the team were older than Crompton, although the majority were only a couple of years his senior.

Crompton's full-back partner, William Taylorson, was born on 28 August 1875 in Higher Audley Street, the son of a Yorkshire mechanic. The family later moved to Eden Street. Taylorson worked as a weaver but died in 1903, when his daughter Margaret was only two. William Norris, the captain, was born in late 1875 in Moss Street, although the family later moved to Walter Street, just off Audley Range. Although he started work as a weaver, he later left town to keep a boarding house in Coronation Street in Blackpool, but returned to Blackburn where he was employed as an electric car driver.

One of the few men who did not work in the mill was John Willis Greenhalgh, born in 1874, the son of a fruit merchant from Burnley. He had been born in Tontine Street, but the family moved around the corner to Bicknell Street. He was a clerk on the railway. The Miller brothers, John (born in 1868) and Thomas (1873), were the sons of John Miller, who kept the Royal Edward Beer House on

Whalley Banks. They were both weavers as was Albert King (born in 1878) of London Road. John Dewhurst, born in Barrow in 1874 but the son of a local man, was a plumber from Audley Range. Frank Wilkinson, who came from Eastwood Street, worked in the warehouse of the cotton mill his father managed.

The star of the team was 'Jud' Brindle (another weaver, born in 1877) who in 1897 at Rishton once ran the entire length of the field with the ball but faced with the goalkeeper realised he was too tired to shoot, drew him from the line and squared it for Dewhurst to walk it home. Brindle's deputy was Edmund Jepson (born in 1873), a bookkeeper from Whalley New Road. At the end of the season Crompton was selected for his first representative honour, chosen for the rest of the Sunday School League against the champions, St Andrew's Mission, at Witton on 11 April 1896. In the game he was one of the most distinguished players, the *Blackburn Times* stating, 'Hereabouts Crompton of the league was playing a grand game at full-back.' In September 1896 Crompton signed for Rovers, although it was to be a further two years before he relinquished his amateur status because of his desire to continue playing water polo.

When Crompton left school, he decided to become a plumber. He took an apprenticeship with William Naylor, a journeyman plumber from Keighley who had chosen not to follow his father, Smith Naylor, in the family firm of spindle finishers. He had moved to Blackburn in the 1870s with his wife and two children and settled in Balaclava Street. Mary Elizabeth died in 1899 and he remarried to Esther Edge, a widow from Chorley who was ten years older than him. The family and Esther's daughter, Lily, moved to a new home in Withers Street.

Crompton's recruitment by Rovers was almost forced upon them because, before the season started, they lost two left-backs who had been in contention for the position in the first team. First, they found that Walter Porter was unlikely to play that season and then Arthur Blackburn seriously injured his foot in the public practice game. This left the position open for their newly imported Scottish player, Hugh Devlin, from Cambuslang. He opened the season, was responsible for the goal that defeated them and said goodbye to his Ewood Park career. Playing in the reserves he suffered a bad injury when Geary of Everton fell on him, but he was a player who attracted misfortune. When he signed for Blackburn he took up lodgings with the club's inside-forward, Harry Campbell. Coming home one afternoon earlier than had been anticipated he found Devlin unconscious. Not used to gas, he had turned it on and up to full but was overcome by the fumes. If Campbell had not returned home early and obtained medical help immediately, Devlin would have perished. As a consequence of the mayhem at the position, Crompton was asked to sign amateur forms, which brought this announcement in the *Blackburn Times*:

'On Wednesday evening [30 September 1896] the Rovers committee signed a new back in a local player named Robert Crompton, who has played for the Blackburn Trinity. Crompton is regarded as a very promising youth.'

Although offered a professional engagement, Crompton declined since it would have affected his status as a water polo player and prevented him playing the game. His signing, though, was not a foregone conclusion. Edgar Chadwick had been brought up in the family bakery at King Street. He had joined Rovers but left for Everton while still a young man because he had been offered greater wages. Since that time he had become an international, but he returned to Blackburn regularly and had spotted that Crompton was a rare talent, even if the view was not universal. He spent a considerable amount of time inducing him to join Everton, the situation being made more critical by the fact that Rovers were somewhat lukewarm about the youngster. At that point John Lewis became acquainted with the situation, stepped in, approached Crompton personally and tied him to Rovers.

On Saturday, 3 October Crompton saw his first action at Ewood Park.

The *Blackburn Times* wrote, 'The reserve teams of Rovers and Darwen met at Ewood on Saturday. Darwen had a powerful 11 which included several of the first team forwards. On the Rovers' side Blackburn turned out for the first time since his injury. Jos Hargreaves also had sufficiently recovered to don the colours and Crompton of Trinity was given a trial.'

The verdict on Crompton was: 'Crompton put in some useful work, particularly in the second half.'

For the first half of the season Crompton partnered Art Blackburn at full-back with the reserves. They became well established, 'tackling fearlessly and well'. In January it was observed, 'Bob Crompton fairly pleased the Preston critics. He played a sound game last Saturday and bottled up young Becton [a future international] in a manner he seldom has been this season.'

Immediately after Christmas, Walter Porter was fit for action and he had seniority over Crompton. The committee, though, had a desire to continue with the youngster and they judged that with his strapping physique and commitment he could be moved to centre-half, to the exclusion of Edward Nuttall. Even when Arthur Blackburn broke down and had to have an operation on his foot, Crompton was not moved to his natural position (Albert Thornber from the Ragged School, signed a few days before Crompton, was brought in) and for the remainder of the season he played at centre-half and appeared to be improving. Meanwhile the first team were in a state of decline, and when Kelly Houlker broke his collarbone, there was concern about the depth of the half-back line. With a free date on 3 April the club arranged a friendly with Darwen, to follow immediately after the reserve game with Preston. The committee decided to look at the newly signed reserve goalkeeper Charles Saer, the future first secretary of the Players' Union, and Crompton.

Rovers: Saer, Brandon, Killean, Booth, Crompton, Anderson, Haydock, Hargreaves, Proudfoot, Wilkie, Campbell.

Darwen: Kingsley, Leach, Howarth, Sharpe, Morrison, Fish, Hunt, Ratcliffe, Lees, Cumpstey, Ashcroft.

The game ended in a 2-2 draw and 'Crompton played a hard game and he showed promise of making a good player', as reported in the *Blackburn Times*. The committee clearly agreed because a week later he was selected to make his debut at Stoke, Geordie Dewar being omitted.

Rovers: Ogilvie, Brandon, Killean, Booth, Crompton, Anderson, Nicol, Tierney, Proudfoot, Wilkie, Campbell.

Stoke: Johnstone, Clare, Eccles, Brodie, Grewer, Rowley, Johnson, Hill, Hingerty, W.S. Maxwell, Schofield.

They lost 1-0 and Crompton's performance was not commented on, but he was retained the following week when Rovers played the final game of the season at Aston Villa. This produced another defeat, 3-0, and Crompton was observed to have been caught flat-footed after only five minutes when Campbell burst past him to score.

The season ended with a Scottish tour, in which Rovers lost two of the three games, and a friendly defeat to Oldham County. The standing of Crompton in the game was placed in perspective when the Rest of the Lancashire Combination side to meet the champions, Preston North End, in April, was selected. It was: Thompson (Burnley), Harper (Manchester City), Handford (Burnley), Chambers (Blackburn Rovers), Wallwork (Turton), Scotchard (Bury; captain), Colvin (Liverpool), Tonge (Manchester City), Cunliffe (Liverpool), Moreland (Blackburn Rovers), Clark (Skelmersdale). Exactly where Crompton stood in the estimation of Rovers' committee was hard to tell but the line-up for the public practice game the following season gave a clue. The vacancy alongside Tom Brandon at full-back had been plugged by the signing of Jack Glover from West Bromwich Albion. With future England international Tom Booth of Ashton North End having developed more rapidly, Crompton was selected for the game as the reserve team centre-half.

First team: A. Knowles, T. Brandon, J. Glover, T. Booth, E. Killean, W. Ball, J. Bradbury, C. Hall, J. Proudfoot, J. Wilkie, H. Campbell.

Reserves: M. Tyson, A. Blackburn, A. Mills, J. Sherrington, R. Crompton, A. Houlker, B. Ling, T. Briercliffe, S.P. Colley, B. Hulse, H. Garstang.

An examination of the career of Crompton's teammates demonstrates just how fecund a footballing nursery the town was.

MATTHEW TYSON
Born: Blackburn, 23 May 1879
Died: Lancaster, 19 April 1945
Tyson was a young local boy, who started with the Ragged School, and later played for Etrurians. He was the son of Joe Tyson, a mill worker from Preston, and was working in the mills before he was a teenager.

ARTHUR BLACKBURN
Born: Billington, 4 June 1876
Died: Trawden, 3 December 1938
Career: Mellor; Blackburn Rovers; St Peter's; Blackburn Trinity; Wellingborough; Blackburn Rovers; Southampton; Blackburn Rovers
Born in Billington, his family moved to Mellor Brow before his second birthday and Art followed his father into the cotton mills, although the father subsequently became landlord of the Windmill Inn and then the Eagle Inn, both in Mellor. Arthur was signed by Rovers but spent most of the next three years playing for local junior clubs until he received an offer from Wellingborough. He soon returned north, recuperating from an ankle injury, and rejoined Rovers at a time when his younger brother, Fred, was starting to play with the first team. He was given his debut and was even selected as a reserve for the Football League against the Irish League. He played well on the last day of the 1899/1900 season, so much so that a representative from Southampton tailed him home and offered him £1 a

week more than Rovers were paying. He was reluctant to leave but Rovers would not match the offer and, because he was out of work and renovating a church as a voluntary worker, financial necessities forced him to move south. He was a huge success with his new club, but an ankle injury hindered his appearances. A year later he was back at Ewood, until he broke his leg in his second game and was forced to retire. He became a coach in Rotterdam and returning to England he bought a herbalist's shop in Rishton.

ANDREW MILLS

Born: Aston on Clun, Shropshire, 15 December 1877
Died: Llandrindod Wells, 1 January 1954
Career: Knighton; Blackburn Rovers; Swindon Town; Brighton United; Leicester Fosse; Shrewsbury Town (trial)

Rovers noticed Andy Mills, a hard-working left-back from Radnorshire, playing in the Welsh international trial, but his signing was one of speculation rather than need. The club had good full-backs so Mills's opportunities were limited, his last coming in the test matches when Killean broke his leg. Immediately Mills sought the more welcoming pastures of the Southern League and the next Rovers heard of him was when Leicester negotiated for his transfer. He was a big success with the Fosse and in 1903 looked to be on his way to a Welsh cap when an impressive international trial was curtailed by a serious leg injury. He scored three goals for Leicester, two penalties and a punt from his own half.

JOHN SHERRINGTON
Born: Higher Walton, 7 April 1877
Died: Blackburn, 27 January 1945
Career: Blackburn Vale; Blackburn Rovers; Darwen; Nelson;Park Road; Great Harwood
At the age of 16 Sherrington signed with Blackburn Vale and in his first season helped them finish as runners-up in the Blackburn Combination. The following year they were champions and at 18 he had signed amateur forms for Rovers. A year later he was a professional and was a hard-working left-half in the side that finished runners-up in the Lancashire Combination. A premature debut saw him struggle and to obtain regular football he moved to Darwen. After a spell away from the game he helped Park Road to the final of the Lancashire Junior Cup. Once again he retired, but Great Harwood tempted him back and in four seasons the club gained honours every year. In 1907 he was granted a benefit for which Rovers sent a side to Great Harwood. He worked as a tramway plater.

ALBERT EDWARD 'KELLY' HOULKER
Born: Blackburn, 27 April 1872
Died: Blackburn, 27 May 1962
Career: Blackburn Hornets; Oswaldtwistle Rovers; Cob Wall; Park Road; Blackburn Rovers; Portsmouth; Southampton; Blackburn Rovers; Colne Internationals: Five England appearances

With a head of dark, tightly curled black hair and a weather-beaten complexion Houlker was often mistaken for an Irishman, which led to his nickname. In fact, he was the son of William Houlker of Carlisle Street and followed his father into the cotton mill where he was a weaver. He played for a series of local clubs but caught the eye of Rovers following a medals competition after which four of the side signed terms with the club. Park Road were known as the Nanny Goats because they trained on goat meat provided by a butcher in the Grimshaw Park area. A perpetual motion player, he served a two-year apprenticeship before becoming a regular but once in the side he caught the eye. When he caught the eye of the England selectors the inevitable happened. Agreement about wages could not be reached and Houlker pursued an illustrious career on the south coast before returning to Ewood for a second spell. He worked as an overlooker at Grange Street Mill before starting his own coal and haulage business. He has the honour of being the oldest man to represent the club, playing in an emergency during wartime football in January 1918. An active Liberal and member of the Reform Club he was born in Dean Street, Blackburn, and died in Downham Street.

BENJAMIN LING
Born: Blackburn, 8 September 1876
Died: North Walsham, December quarter 1951
Ling's grandfather, Lewis, farmed 37 acres in Oakley in Suffolk but hardships in the agricultural industry forced

his son, Levi, to move to Blackburn to work at the Star paper mill. Benjamin was born in the Livesey area and was employed as a clerk at the mill. He had a reputation locally as a sprinter, and a dashing winger with Cherry Tree before he signed for Rovers in 1897. He played on the Star side that won the National Union of Paper Mill Operatives Cup in 1904 and 1905. On both occasions Star beat Turnlees of Glossop.

THOMAS 'CHIP' BRIERCLIFFE
Born: Blackburn, 16 May 1874 (baptised 14 June 1874)
Died: Blackburn, 18 February 1948
Career: St Luke's; Wheelton; Rawtenstall; Bacup; Clitheroe; Blackburn Rovers; Stalybridge Rovers; Woolwich Arsenal; Plymouth Argyle; Brentford; Darwen

The son of a fish and fruit merchant from Galligreaves Road, 'Chip' Briercliffe had a variety of occupations, among them carter and hod carrier, in several Lancashire towns. He made the grade the hard way playing for local clubs before signing for Rovers, at a time when he had a dislocated shoulder. He quickly became a firm favourite, running the wing with bounce and displaying an eye for goal but he was unfortunate that Fred Blackburn came along to displace him. After the obscurity of Stalybridge, he joined Arsenal and served them for several seasons during which he helped them to gain promotion to the First Division. A reserve for England, he gained county caps for London and Devon, although his time in the West Country was cut short when he obtained the tenancy of the Infirmary Hotel in Blackburn. This occupation proved ideal and he moved to several public houses, the last of which was the Royal Oak in Highfield Road. He was the brother-in-law of Everton's William Stevenson, the pair having married sisters.

SAMUEL PEARSON COLLEY

Born: Fleetwood, September quarter 1871 (baptised 3 March 1872)

Died: Fleetwood, June quarter 1955

Colley was a Fleetwood fisherman who could play in virtually every outfield position for Fleetwood Rangers. He might have become a star in the Football League but had a troublesome knee which limited his appearances. He signed for Rovers in 1897 but made only a few reserve appearances. His father, who had the same name, moved up from Stoke with his stepfather John Wright and became a fisherman, eventually skippering Excelsior. Despite the dangers of the profession, he didn't die until the age of 82 and his son exceeded that by a year. In 1895 Colley junior was rescued when the smack in which he was sailing, *Genesta*, collided with the paddle steamer *Greyhound* during a fierce storm. In January 1938 he was skipper of the yacht *Defender* which, after night fishing in the Irish Sea, was returning up the River Wyre when it was struck by a trawler and sank. Two men were drowned, one of them being Jimmy Hampson, the Blackpool and England centre-forward.

BENJAMIN DANIEL HULSE
Born: Liverpool, 3 August 1875
Died: Liverpool, 30 May 1950
Career: Liverpool South End; Rock Ferry; New Brighton
Tower; Blackburn Rovers; New Brighton Tower; Millwall;
Brighton & Hove Albion; Brynn Central; Ashton Town;
Eccles Borough (trial)
A tall, lithe player who could use the ball constructively
and score goals he turned professional at the age of 15.
His family had lived in hardship after his father died when
he was five and his mother worked as a laundress to bring
up the family in the Toxteth Park area. During his years
with his first club, they climbed from the Liverpool and
District League to the Lancashire Combination, which
attracted the attentions of larger local
clubs. He signed for New Brighton but
at the time they were not affiliated
to the FA and Rovers profited by
stepping in and signing him. After a
slow start he established himself and
became a regular goalscorer. When
the talented Peter Somers arrived,
Hulse's place was in jeopardy and
terms were agreed with Everton.
Objections at the Merseysiders' annual
general meeting held up the deal and Hulse signed instead
for New Brighton who were now in the Football League.
A move to Millwall followed New Brighton's collapse
and, converted to centre-forward, Hulse scored 35 goals
in 60 games. He ended his career playing as a full-back
in the Lancashire Combination.

HARRY GARSTANG

Born: Salford, 7 June 1875
Died: Blackburn, 13 February 1959

Garstang's grandparents John and Charlotte Dixon farmed 46 acres at Shadsworth Villas. For a time John owned Ewood Park, when it was a racecourse. Daughter Sarah Jane married a Manchester man and their first two children, Harry and John, were born in Salford. Not long after, her husband died and Sarah returned to live with her grandparents, where a third son, Charles, was born. Sarah subsequently married a licensee, James Eddleston, who had managed the Armenia Cotton Mill, and their families moved to the Albion Inn in Bolton Street, Lower Darwen. After an education at Whalley Grammar School, Harry trained as an electrical engineer and started to play in the forward line for Blackburn Etrurians. In 1897, after helping Etrurians win the Lancashire Amateur Cup, he signed for Rovers and made an immediate impact with the reserves. In the Christmas holiday game with Accrington he broke his leg when he fell in an icy pitch. He never recovered and had to retire from the game.

During 1898 Harry's work took him to Warwickshire, but he eventually returned to Blackburn to set up as a motor engineer in Mincing Lane. He prospered so well that in 1904 he was elected to Rovers' board and except for a break of 12 months he served as a director for 21 years. Once serving as a linesman at a reserve game he stopped the play until he had admonished a foul-mouthed heckler. Although he was 16 years older than his wife

Clara, he outlived her by a couple of years. He lived in Preston New Road when he retired and was living in St Silas Road at the time of his death, in the infirmary. He held the fourth licence to drive a car issued in Blackburn and owned one of the early steam-driven cars. During the war he designed and built an X-ray machine for use in the hospital in Blackburn.

* * *

Before the season commenced the team arranged a friendly against Burnley, who had just been relegated. They lost 3-1 and consequently Kelly Houlker, who had played at left-half, was left out when the season commenced at Derby. Killean moved to take his place and Crompton was brought in. It was not a happy return to the colours.

'Crompton was often in difficulty and when his confreres went to his aid it gave the opposite side a complete advantage,' said the *Blackburn Times*.

Houlker recovered his place, Crompton went back to the reserves and, even though Rovers were in such poor form that they finished at the bottom of the table and had to undergo the dreaded test matches, Crompton saw no first-team action. Despite losing both full-backs, Brandon and Killean, during these four games, Rovers did not bring him in, instead playing Glover and the Welshman Andy Mills. With his football career stalling, Crompton was undoubtedly grateful that he had held on to his amateur status. On the Thursday following his game on the opening day of the season he was in the Blackburn Corporation Baths, playing with the town water polo team against Bacup Madena. After his struggles on the football field, it was no doubt cathartic to display his prowess. He scored five goals in the team's 8-1 win, even though he played at half-back and not in the forwards.

Despite their failure in the test matches, Rovers were handed a reprieve when the Football League was extended and they kept their place in the top flight. Before the season it was announced that it had been decided that Crompton's future lay at full-back, although his absence from the public practice games was not commented upon. Brandon and Glover (who had arrived from West Bromwich Albion in May 1897) were back as the first-team backs and the reserves were a couple of new men, Charles Brown from Leith Athletic and Richard Hornby from Park Road. Although it was not noted it is likely that Crompton was unfit because after the team had commenced the season badly with a defeat at Everton, Crompton replaced the injured Glover at left-back. It was noted in the *Blackburn Times*, 'Crompton, after the first few minutes, settled down to steady play and gave a very satisfactory account of himself.'

Granted a run of games, Crompton made the position his own and soon club and player were happy enough for him to relinquish his amateur status and start taking wages, although they were considerably less than the £4-a-week maximum. The club appeared so convinced about the young man that they let Glover join Liverpool. The following season saw a significant development in his career. His full-back partner had always been the Scottish international, Tom Brandon, a man who played football with cavalier disregard and had a private life that was catching up with him. He had started an affair with a local woman and deserted his family to live with her. Not long afterwards he was in court for failure to provide for his wife and children.

He fled for St Mirren, where his brother was a player but stayed only briefly before leaving for the United States. He had joined Rovers in 1889 but, although he left for The Wednesday in 1891, he returned to the club in December 1893 and had been the first-choice right-back ever since. With Crompton he had struck up a fine understanding and his loss was a grievous one.

To compensate, Rovers moved Crompton to his natural position for the first time since his debut two and a half years previously and brought in Allen Hardy at left-back. A miner from Ilkeston, Hardy had come north to play cricket as a professional for Wigan but his footballing performances at left-back for Wigan County had caught Rovers' eye. The move was opportune for Crompton who on the opening day of the season had failed to cope with the wiles of the great Billy Meredith, although he was far from being the only left-back to struggle against the Welshman.

Although Hardy struggled initially the pair settled and the consolidation of Rovers as a sound mid-table side continued. Off the field Crompton and the committee had their differences. From their formation the discipline of the players had proved troublesome. In the early days it was the arrogance of the sons of the gentry, who resented being omitted and playing in bad weather, that created problems. They were of such magnitude that the founder, John Lewis, once quit the club and joined Darwen in protest. He returned to play a key role in the administration as football ushered in professionalism.

Although Rovers were at the forefront of the drive to remunerating the players, they were no advocates of total professionalism. Lewis and one of his successors, Dr E.S. Morley, contended that players should be compensated for loss of earnings through their dedication to the game but that no man should have a living only based on football. This stance rebounded on them spectacularly when more and more of the players became licensees. At first it had appeared an ideal situation, but they soon found the downside. International players like Hugh McIntyre and Joe Lofthouse grew distinctly corpulent and increasingly unfit, combining the two occupations. Lofthouse received the nickname 'Guinness's Porter' for his over-indulgence. Worse still, their head for business was not good and the pair and another Rovers great, Fergie Suter, all ran their establishments into insolvency.

At the club's annual general meeting in 1892, member George Lewis asked to put forward a motion that 'no playing member of the club be allowed to keep a public house'. A seconder for the motion was found but the wily chairman, Dr Morley, declared that the meeting was already wound up and the matter would have to be carried forward to the next one. Amid uproar, Joe Lofthouse pointed out that Jimmy Brown had kept a public house for ten years and he was not a bad player. Another committee man, Henry Ibbotson, attempted to defuse the situation by putting forward the motion that 'a player could do whatever he wished', pointing out that the question of individuals' fitness was a matter for the committee. Morley declined to accept this motion on similar grounds to the Lewis proposal and the meeting broke up in some confusion and ill feeling. Lewis was not a relation of John Lewis, but he was a man who regularly provided lodgings for the Scottish players who signed for Rovers.

The meeting effectively prevented the club from taking a dictatorial attitude, although their concern was not without precedent. A pen picture of the Darwen, Burnley and Bolton full-back Tom Woolfall noted that he 'is one of the footballers who can manage a licensed house and still play a good game'. Rovers also had misgivings about Crompton's apprenticeship as a plumber and glazier, a job he worked in regularly when he was not required to train. Despite the heavy nature of the work, Rovers' ability to dictate his choice of employment was not strong since he was not on the maximum wage. Another Rovers player, Josh Hargreaves, had been a full-time weaver, which was not exactly a sinecure of a job, but the feeling was that it was not as dangerous as plumbing.

Just before Christmas of 1900 the situation came to a head. On 17 December, a Monday morning, Crompton was installing a plate glass window when the glass broke, penetrating his wrist and severing arteries. He set off on foot to find a doctor but most of them were out on their rounds and he had lost a great deal of blood before he finally obtained medical help. He missed a month's football, including all of the Christmas and New Year games. Rovers were concerned and Crompton himself had his reservations, but his form did not suffer and in February he was called up for the international trial as a late replacement, although unfortunately at left-back, rather than on the right.

North: Kingsley (Newcastle United), Balmer (Everton), Crompton (Blackburn Rovers), Wolstenholme (Everton), Crawshaw (Sheffield Wednesday), Needham (Sheffield United), Johnston (Stoke City), Bloomer (Derby County), Hedley (Sheffield United), Bull (Notts County), Cox (Liverpool).

South: Robinson (Southampton), W.J. Oakley (Corinthians), C.B. Fry (Corinthians), H. Vickers (Casuals), Hitch (QPR), Jones (Bristol City), Richard (Bury), R.E. Foster (Old Malvernians), R.N.R. Blaker (Cambridge University), Banks (Millwall), B.O. Corbett (Corinthians).

Opinions on Crompton's performance varied but the consensus was that he was as good as any back and might have been considerably better if he had received more support from the wing-half in front of him, the veteran international Ernest Needham. *The Times* was quite clear, 'Of the backs Crompton was best.'

In normal circumstances he might have expected an international call-up, but the trial had been hit by withdrawals in the South's forward line, so Crompton's immediate opponent was a player from Bury. Ultimately the selectors went with the status quo for the first international, but there was a body of opinion that thought he might be required for either of the next two games. That was soon an academic matter. Playing against Derby County he fell in a heap with Jack Arkesden and was helped off with a broken rib and several displaced ones. It terminated his season and sent him into a close-season of discontent.

Reports of Crompton leaving the club had first arisen in November 1899 when a Tyneside newspaper carried a report that Rovers had offered Crompton and Ben Hulse to Newcastle. Rovers' committee laughed off the story but privately Crompton might have felt that there may have been some truth in the offer. Hulse's position at the club was in some doubt because of the arrival of Jack Dewhurst from Darwen, and it could not have escaped Crompton's notice that Rovers had signed Allen Hardy in the close-season. The feeling was that the report had some substance as Rovers sought to raise finance. With the prominence of an international trial to his credit it was anticipated that he would be the target for other clubs. It was an open secret that Everton, who had regularly enticed good players like Edgar Chadwick and Jack Southworth away from the club, had been in contact with him.

Rovers conceded that Crompton's contract entitled him to a free transfer and confirmed that he had asked for his release. They countered by offering the maximum wage of £4 a week and declared that this prevented any club contacting him and, if they found that he was negotiating, any club concerned would be guilty of an illegal approach. Crompton had given his reasons for wanting to leave, stating that he had not been fairly treated by the spectators in the last few matches, a strange remark since he missed the final five games. It was known that he was unhappy about the opinions of the crowd when he severed his arteries. The popular Bob Howarth was moved from centre-half to cover for him and rollicking Sam McClure (ironically destined to become Crompton's brother-in-law) was brought in. Howarth and McClure were huge friends and loved by the crowd and there were plenty who hoped that neither would lose his place when Crompton recovered.

By the first week of August Crompton was still not signed, but he married Ada Ingham at the end of July and commenced married life in a public house, the Queen's Hotel, he had taken over in Audley Range. It was part of the way along, at the junction with Cherry Street, and is still standing, although it is now used by a supplier for barbecues. There was plenty of competition locally with the Audley Arms and the Lord Howard Arms in the same street, but it was a large property with 12 rooms and gave scope for letting rooms as well as serving alcohol. By then the signs were obvious that Crompton had accepted the club's terms and that he was also going to spend less time with the blow lamp and more behind the bar. Crompton finished his apprenticeship and was offered and accepted a partnership. Although he reduced his plumbing work, he was by no means a sleeping partner and the business was to drastically alter his life.

Crompton was not back in harness when the first public practice game was staged but he was when the second game was held. He was also made team captain. His appointment marked a sea change in Rovers' achievements. They finished fourth and gained silverware when they beat Burnley in the Lancashire Senior Cup Final. Crompton was a towering figure.

'Next to the great custodian [Jack Hillman of Burnley] in order of merit was Bob Crompton whose fearless tackling and splendid kicking were features of the match,' wrote the *Northern Daily Telegraph*.

In March Crompton was invited to the England trial, this time in his correct position. On 8 March he made his England debut against Wales. The following week he played against Ireland. By common consensus he played well but the fact that he gave away a penalty in both games meant that his selection for the big one, against Scotland, was problematic. The selectors held faith and Crompton rewarded them.

The *Lancashire Daily Post* reported, 'Crompton's maiden effort against Scotland was in every way excellent. He tackled the fine left-winger Alec Smith with telling effect.

His Gibraltar like defence stood out as a bulwark among a band of mighty men. Well may Lancashire feel proud of this, one of her finest sons.'

A year after he had made his debut, Crompton was invited to captain his country on 2 March 1903.

There were few who understood Crompton's compulsion for business when his football career was going so well. It was a characteristic that placed him apart from his teammates but had a precedent. A predecessor as a Rovers fullback, Johnny Murray, had displayed a similar ability to look beyond the immediate. When the Scottish international joined from Sunderland, two years after leaving Scotland, he only made the move when he obtained a full-time job. Whereas most players sought what they believed was the sinecure of the tenancy of an inn, Murray looked to the future. He applied for a post as engraver at Brinscall Calico Works and once there worked his way up to be head engraver. When his two occupations conflicted, he chose security over glory and retired from football, a year before Crompton signed for Rovers. Even with his international career blossoming Crompton spent his time away from the club in expanding his business interests. If few of his clubmates understood he could soon tangibly demonstrate the wisdom of his actions. He and his partner, William Naylor, invented, built and patented a flushing tank that had huge implications for the providers of water supplies. Crompton himself explained the device:

'We claim, my partner and I, that wherever there is a big force of water, other cisterns will not cut off after the flush thus causing a continual waste of water. Our invention, however, always cuts off completely the moment the cistern is empty, and it is this fact which has recommended it to the corporation [Blackburn] besides which it is simple in construction and less liable to get out of order than any other. The technical name for it is a patent siphon water waste prevention cistern.'

At the start of 1905 the national newspapers got wind of the story and claimed that Crompton had been offered £2,000 by the Blackburn Corporation for the patent rights. It caused a sensation because it was a huge amount of money. Even split equally with his partner, it was the equivalent of five years of his football earnings, but the story was not totally correct, although the ultimate benefit to Crompton was likely to make him a rich man, as he acknowledged. Blackburn Corporation had examined the invention and had decided that only that and one other make would be installed in the borough but had not made an offer for the patent.

Crompton told the *Blackburn Times*, 'We are doing very well indeed with it and that it is a very good thing which may be worth more to us than the figure quoted. There have been many inquiries from outside about it and we shall cover the neighbouring towns as soon as we have finished with Blackburn.'

Notwithstanding his newfound affluence, Crompton continued to be the landlord of the Queen's Hotel. There was an all too obvious sign of his prosperity. Soon after the launch of his sanitary miracle he acquired a motor car. The cost of a Humber at the time was about £1,000, although other makes had a price as high as £1,500. The type of car is hard to identify from remaining evidence, but its design was similar to a Humber. It may have been that it was a Leander, manufactured by James Walmsley at his carriage works in Preston. In buying a car Crompton became the first footballer to obtain one. His reasoning was simple. He had ridden motorcycles from his youth but with an expanding family it made sense to indulge himself from his newfound wealth. Initially it caused little comment locally but in other towns there was some degree of incredulity that a footballer had joined the ranks of the gentry in acquiring motorised transport. A Nottingham newspaper of October 1905 carried this report:

'It is not generally known that Crompton, the Blackburn full-back, is a player of an inventive disposition and has just made a large fortune by an invention. He now drives up to his training quarters in a motor car.'

Crompton used the *Blackburn Times* to deny that he had made a fortune but confirmed he was now a motorist. It was only the start of what became the saga of Bob Crompton and his motor car. Cars were mechanically unreliable, and Crompton's driving appears to have been somewhat cavalier. His range of mishaps, many of which might have proved fatal, was an open secret at the club. Finally, his propensity for accident could not be concealed. One wintry night he was returning from Preston accompanied by his brother-in-law, Sam McClure, when his steering gear jammed. A lamp post loomed ahead, and the car destroyed it, and itself. The two men climbed unhurt from the wreckage but found that, with the last train gone, they had to walk the ten miles to Blackburn. Whereas the ever-cheerful McClure undertook the walk with a smile and a spring in his step, it is known that Crompton was still grumbling as they finally sighted home. Some enterprising locals who knew Crompton's previous driving history and could not see him dodging the odds forever thought of a way to profit. They sought insurance brokers, who sold them policies based on Crompton's life. The reasoning was that the way Crompton conducted a motor car, they would have few annual premiums to pay before they collected.

Crompton did go missing from the line-up at the start of 1905, although it was a sprained knee not a motoring mishap that caused his absence. At least at Blackburn he received the best in medical technology. A former player, Harry Garstang, had been elected to the board of directors the previous year. He was an engineer who had a motor engineering business but was among the pioneers on the field of radiography. He had built his own machine and when Crompton was improving little he was examined by the latest medical asset. The news was that there was 'something strange in the appearance of bones at the ankle joint'. Although Dr Craven, the club doctor, was unsure whether this was another injury, it was of sufficient concern for the club to send him to the Manchester specialist, Dr Collier, who eventually effected a cure for the problems. It was too late for the 1905 Home International tournament, but he was back on the field by the end of the season and in the summer of 1905 it appeared that few men were more touched by fortune than Crompton. He had become the captain of his country and there were those who claimed that he was the best footballer in the world. His plumbing business was producing an income far greater than his maximum wage as a footballer, and he had become one of the few motorists of the times. His wife was expecting their third child. True, the family had been having concerns about the health of his brother-in-law Sam McClure, who had been absent from football since January with an undiagnosed illness that had caused him to lose much weight. His health had improved, and he was preparing during the summer months to get fit enough to resume playing.

The Cromptons' child, Thomas, was born in the summer but he lived only a few weeks. The day before Thomas died, Bob insisted on fulfilling his duties to Rovers, playing against Notts County although he knew how seriously ill his son was. The death affected Crompton more than anyone might have realised but the committee and players allowed him to grieve privately and sought the co-operation of the local reporters, 'Ranger' and 'Perseus', to suppress the story. There was no comment made about his absence from the pre-season public practice games and nor did they disclose that he had resigned the captaincy of the team to deal with his family's grief. It was not until on the opening day of the season, when goalkeeper Bob Evans went forward for the coin toss, that his decision became known. Even then there was no information disclosed for his reasons.

Fortunately, McClure was back in the team to help Crompton through trying times. The aloof, diffident Crompton had found in McClure his diametric opposite. He had moved down from Workington in April 1899 with a winning smile, a thousand stories and a larger repertoire of jokes. He had become a legend in his youth in Cumberland, as at home in the water as he was on land. He was an intrepid sailor, tireless rower and able swimmer. At the summer fairs he was a champion sprinter but in team games he was an indefatigable warhorse. In Workington, his Saturday schedule was football in the morning, rugby in the afternoon and football again at night, all competitive games. On the football field he played anywhere for his team, Black Diamonds. He had signed for Everton the previous year as a goalkeeper but arrived at Ewood alternating between the half-back line and goal. A second-generation Irishman, his parents John and Eliza had moved to Harrington, lured by the prospects of work. Universally liked, he had no enemies, although he was an implacable opponent who would back down to no one. At a time when the game was violent, he ranked among the hardest, but he gave and took in equal measure and greeted everything with a smile that brought him a thousand friendships.

Life is unpredictable and these two diverse personalities married sisters, who were born a year apart. Ada and Bertha Ingham were daughters of Thomas Ingham, a Preston man who was a potato merchant who lived in Ainsworth Street. Ada, the eldest, married Crompton; Bertha wed McClure. How two genetically similar women could opt for two such different types can only be explained by the utter randomness of love.

McClure had apparently overcome his illness but in the close-season he returned to spend time in Workington, where he was taken ill. An abscess in his ear spread inwards to the brain and he died before surgery could be performed. He was only 29 years old. The symptoms suggest that the illness was a cholesteatoma, where a polyp forms at the end of the Eustachian tube and creates enzymes which erode the mastoid bone and everything else in the area. It can be arrested by surgery but there was little experience of this at the time. His death was a massive blow for Crompton who had never enjoyed a close friendship with any other team-mate.

The hurt in Crompton's life was ameliorated by his love of motoring. He had continued to produce plumbing innovations and had taken out further patents, but none was as overwhelmingly lucrative as his first. It became apparent that his income from football, public house and plumbing was not going to maintain his standard of living as a motorist. Ever the pragmatist, Crompton commenced in 1906 to build his own motor car, larger and more powerful than the one he owned. Such enterprise attracted the attention and approval of a team-mate. William Davies signed for Rovers in April 1905 from Wrexham. He was two years younger than Crompton and had served an apprenticeship in an engineering works. The death of his father when he was 17 left him as sole breadwinner for a family of seven, which his weekly wage of 14 shillings and sixpence would not cover. Proud and resourceful, he took to the roads selling pots and pans, which brought him the nickname of 'Tinker'.

The similarities between the men were marked and Crompton made use of Davies's engineering skills. The pair commenced to spend their spare time working on Crompton's new car. In 1910 their hobby turned into a commercial enterprise which forced Crompton to turn down an FA tour of South Africa. Their motor engineering business would not permit him to be absent for over a month. Shrewdly in 1912 the couple hired as their foreman Sam Isherwood, an experienced mechanic who worked for Rawlinson's in Audley Range. Curiously in a Blackpool court in 1917, when driving one of the company's lorries he had famously collided with a tram, Isherwood stated that he had been driving for Crompton for 15 years. By the time he left to work for himself in 1919, the business was well established.

The partnership of Crompton and Davies lasted for 20 years, blossoming into a dealership. After the war they opened a showroom in Sudell Cross and obtained the agency for north-east and north-west Lancashire for the 12.5hp Metallurgique car that had a Van Den Plas body. Davies adopted Lancashire as his home and in March 1917 he returned on leave from service with the Mechanical Transport Corps in Malta to marry Edith Cotton, daughter of Clement Cotton, who was in partnership with his brother Lawrence in a highly profitable cotton manufacturing business. Lawrence was chairman of the Rovers. Crompton was ever an active participant in his business. When in September 1919 there was a national rail strike, he drove the company's charabanc to return the Arsenal team, who had been playing at Ewood, home to London. He then picked up a return load, the Burnley team that had been playing Chelsea.

Not everything Crompton touched turned to gold and he never repeated the success of his first plumbing patent. This perhaps coloured his judgement as Rovers' trainer, Moy Atherton, could ruefully testify. When he obtained his position in 1913, Atherton became interested in producing football boots that gave a better grip. He started to use all kind of materials, including canvas covering, but was probably the first man to pioneer rubber screw-in studs. Eventually he settled on an all-weather attachment which consisted of two rubber strips, each with two studs moulded on. Atherton approached Crompton, who had experience of patents, and asked him if he should try to obtain one. Weighing up the cost of such a venture against the uncertainty of identifying the target market and the problems of setting up an operation, Crompton advised against it. Years later, Puma and Adidas successfully marketed similar products and Atherton always regretted not having taken out the patent.

During almost his entire playing career, Crompton retained his tenancy of the Queen's Hotel. He relinquished it in 1914, the licence being transferred to his brother James, who had succeeded his father at the Rose and Thistle, on 5 August. The hotel later passed to one of Crompton's full-back partners, Tommy Suttie. Crompton bought a house in town and moved away from Audley Range. During this time he not only had to play in league and cup games but he was a regular choice in honours matches. In 1913/14 he played in the three Home Internationals, twice represented the Football League against the Scottish League and also against the Irish League, took part in two international trials and the Professionals v Amateurs game. He also turned out in benefit matches for T.E. Harris and Ben Warren.

Such devotion came at a cost. On the morning of Christmas Day 1914 he received the news of the death of his father, who had spent the last days of his life in retirement at Blackpool. Duty came first to Crompton, and he fulfilled the afternoon fixture with Aston Villa before leaving for the coast. Rovers excused him the Boxing Day fixture as well as the New Year's Day and 2 January fixtures. When the Football League was closed in 1915 because of the war, Crompton was 36, but he was able to devote more time to his football than at any time in the previous ten years.

'Tinker' Davies had retired to take a leading role in their motor engineering business and Crompton felt he still had years of football ahead. Unfortunately, it would not be with Rovers in the foreseeable future. The directors had decided that it was unseemly to continue to play football while war raged and refused to participate in wartime matches. Rovers' players were at liberty to guest for other clubs and a group of them, including Crompton, Latheron and Hodkinson, elected to turn out for Blackpool. In February, Rovers conceded that the decision to withdraw from football had been a mistake and they summoned their available players back to training. Over Easter two games were arranged with Newcastle but Crompton had business commitments and did not appear. In August, the club arranged a public practice game in readiness for a season in the wartime league, although first they had to recover Ewood Park from the headquarters it had become for the equine members of the horse artillery. There were strange names among the players and some familiar ones.

Blues: N. Cotton, R. Crompton, W. Pickup, A. Walmsley, P. Smith, W. Bradshaw, A. Longworth, S. Wadsworth, T. Mackereth, R. Green, A. Walsh.

Reds: H. Atkinson, P. Fish, F. Duckworth, M. Proos, G. Chapman, F. Duxbury, A. McGhie, K .Hewitt, R. Morris, E .Latheron, H. Rothwell.

With only seven regulars available the line-ups were completed by local amateurs – two of them, Cotton and Walsh, being the sons of directors. There was also Albert Marinus Proos, born in the Netherlands but raised in Darwen, who was strictly speaking the club's first foreign player. Percy Fish became the greatest athlete Blackburn had ever produced, nationally ranked in both shot and discus. Tom Mackereth was the son of Hartley Mackereth, an old Accrington player who had played for Lancashire. Duckworth and Wadsworth were two youngsters signed by Rovers before the war. Duckworth played in wartime internationals for his country, but Wadsworth went further and became a full international.

Crompton appeared regularly for the first half of the season, and on 2 December had his one and only experience of playing in the forward line, on the right wing against Bury. Soon his business interests began increasingly to make him unavailable. He had returned to spending more time at his motor engineering business and had purchased an interest in a picture house, which was probably the Alexandra Hall in Higher Eanam, which had been opened by the Pendleton Brothers and was known locally as Penks. Opened in 1906, it may have been the country's first purpose-built cinema. The following season Crompton informed the club that he would not have time to play in away matches and his appearances became more infrequent. Whenever he could he looked in and accompanied them to Manchester City where the inexperienced Rovers were reduced to ten men. Adversity brought out the best in the pre-war reserve inside-forward Johnny Orr, who was indefatigable in a lost cause. It also brought out the best in Crompton, who in the company of the secretary Bob Middleton, rushed on to the pitch at the end to congratulate Orr and applaud him all the way back to the dressing room.

3

Bringing honours to Blackburn

WHEN ROVERS only escaped relegation to the Second Division in 1898 because of a decision to add two clubs to the First Division, it had forced the committee to seriously examine the way the club was run. They acknowledged that the dressing room contained a few dubious characters and determined to remedy it. Privately, though, they acknowledged that they also faced problems of lack of success. The last time they had won the FA Cup was in 1891 and, although their record of winning the cup five times made them unique, time soon erases the memory and there was no longer as much desire to play for the club. They had found that the city clubs, particularly Everton, could supply plenty of incentives to attract their best players.

A concentrated effort, headed by one of the famous Chadwick family, Walter, was made to recruit the best local talent. In 1898 the careers of Bob Crompton, Bob Haworth and Fred Blackburn were launched. They also recruited in the unknown area of Workington and came back with Dan Hurst, Peter Chambers, and later Sam McClure. Consequently, they finished sixth in the league, the best position since 1895. It was hard to maintain momentum and, apart from a fourth-placed finish in 1902, the club returned to a mid-table mediocrity.

Redemption came in March 1905 when Lawrence Cotton was elected chairman. He and his brother, Clement, had left Blackburn Grammar School and, after learning the rudiments of the cotton trade, built up their own company to the extent that they became extraordinarily rich. Lawrence was prepared to put some of his money into the business of transforming the town team and instructed the secretary, Bob Middleton, to start bringing in some rising stars. The Welsh international William Davies was the first, but the management pair were cautious, and recruits were few and far between. From a results point of view there was little difference in Rovers' standing.

On other hand the career of Bob Crompton reached new heights and he was considered the finest footballer in the world. Inevitably conjecture started about when Crompton might obtain a team medal. Footballers of the day were far less sanguine about the need for silverware and there were few examples of players who demanded moves so they could obtain medals. Crompton was such a dominant figure in British football that a feeling grew of him deserving to win something. By now he was so embedded in Rovers that the question of him joining more affluent rivals never arose. A belief had arisen that a small-town club like Blackburn could not become champions of the Football League because their resources would never match those of the clubs from cities and large towns. From October 1909 until the first week in January 1910, Rovers had led the First Division until they lost to the eventual champions, Aston Villa. Eventually they finished third. It mirrored Crompton's first experience of fighting for the title ten years before. In 1901/02 the team had given it their best shot.

Mediocre seasons had promised and achieved little, but the team had been strengthened by some judicious additions. After years of inadequate goalkeeping Rovers brought in Walter Whittaker, a Manchester man signed from Reading. A player who had wandered in the hope of finding top-class fame, he was a big man, commanding and confident, who made a significant improvement to the team's morale. Pure class always helps a team and there was no doubt that the Scottish inside-forward Peter Somers provided that. An experienced player, he was skilled in bringing into play the talents of his team-mates. They were shrewd signings because the club had struck a rare vein with their local talent. Crompton, Fred Blackburn and Kelly Houlker became internationals. Arnold Whittaker from Accrington and Jack Dewhurst from Darwen came within isolated votes of achieving that status. The close friends Sam McClure and Bob Haworth were young, vigorous and highly versatile and there was another veteran Scot, Hugh Morgan, who could help Somers orchestrate the situation.

They were aided by an off-field camaraderie that helped during those nights spent in hotels on their travels. Somers was an accomplished pianist who would flex his fingers all evening. Haworth provided vocal accompaniment with equal durability and McClure could always be entreated to perform a step dance. The younger players grew accustomed to being asked to provide a song. They became a team who enjoyed being together.

The season commenced inauspiciously. Rovers were unbeaten in the first three games but won only once. This was followed with three successive losses. The last, at

Grimsby, saw the patience of the directors stretched and inadvertently turned the season around. Walter Whittaker had played for Grimsby and the reception he received was regal. Overcome by the warmth of his greeting he asked the directors if he could stay the night in the town and not return home on the train with the party. Dissatisfied with the performance of the team, the directors were not in accommodating mood and refused his request. Considering the gesture unreasonable, Whittaker missed the train. Interviewed by the directors on his belated return he was unrepentant, aware that the club had spent several seasons searching for a goalkeeper of his class.

There was some surprise when Whittaker was relegated to the reserves because the man promoted was Billy McIver, a tiny goalkeeper in a position where height and weight were given essentials. Whittaker never played for the club again and the agility of McIver contributed to the club finding their feet. The Scottish inside men used the speed of their young wingers to produce devastatingly fast counter-attacks and, provided with the service, Jack Dewhurst plundered goals. By the start of March their ascent of the league was such that they were only three points behind the leaders, Sunderland, who were the next visitors to Ewood. They had also retained the Lancashire Cup. The team had been in the north-east when a telegram arrived from the secretary Joe Walmsley, stating that he had lost the toss for choice of venue, and they had to oppose Everton at Goodison Park. A member of the team was ill-advised enough to express his thoughts. 'Oh, hang,' but he quailed when a glowering Crompton turned on him.

'What's up? We shall win all right,' and they did, courtesy of a goal from Hugh Morgan.

The game against Sunderland was clearly the fixture that would decide the destiny of the league title. Unfortunately, it served to demonstrate why informed opinion believed that a club like the Rovers would not win the championship. Sam McClure had received a kick on the knee in a victory at Everton the previous week and, although hopes had been high, he was not judged fit enough to play. Before the season started they had lost Jimmy Moir, who had a knee problem and a nostalgia for Scotland, and the half-back line had little cover. Billy Bryant, a hard-working if pedestrian inside-forward, was selected to fill the centre-half position because the club simply had no reserve depth.

Rovers: McIver, Crompton, Hardy, Haworth, Bryant, Houlker, Whittaker, Somers, Dewhurst, Morgan, Blackburn.

Sunderland: Doig, McCombie, Watson, Ferguson, McAllister, Jackson, Maxwell, Hewitt, Miller, McLatchie, Gemmell.

The anticipation locally was huge and the attendance of 26,000 exceeded all expectations. Rovers started quickly, and it was soon obvious that Fred Blackburn might be the match-winner. His succession of centres had the defenders working frantically to deal with the danger. On one occasion, Blackburn cut in and his low drive struck the post. Somers then forced Doig to save but Sunderland were not the champions-elect for no reason. They counter-attacked and squared the ball across the goal. Crompton reacted quickly but the bounce of the ball confounded him and Gemmell stole in and whipped the ball into the corner of the net. In the second half Rovers attacked furiously but the defence was strong and, although severely tested, held. Although record gate receipts of £606 were a consolation the club were left to ponder what difference a fit McClure might have made. There was no finer physical specimen in football than McClure and the giant Sunderland defenders would have had a far different proposition in him rather than Bryant, who finished the game battered and bruised from the attentions of the ex-Glasgow Rangers man Miller. A week later their lingering hopes were ended by defeat at Small Heath. Crompton and Houlker were absent playing for the Football League and the squad simply could not shrug off their loss.

The FA Cup appeared to be Crompton's best bet for honours. Unfortunately, season after season Rovers came unstuck before their run had gained any momentum. As Crompton reached 30 and the clock kept ticking, a national desire to see him lift the cup attained momentum, as it did for the immortal Stanley Matthews in 1953. Even the guarded Crompton had not been able to disguise his hopes. In 1911 the dream came to near reality. The problem was that the great man was ageing.

'Quite as much could hardly be said for Crompton who needs to play himself into form. The great back tackled well but he ballooned the ball repeatedly and his placing forward left something to be desired. Still, he is a fine player and although there are those who would have it that he is slower than of yore he is good enough for my money any time,' wrote *Cricket and Football Field*.

The *Northern Daily Telegraph* added, 'His previous displays have evidenced a falling off and one would have liked to have seen him capped once or twice more so as to beat Bloomer's record.'

Meanwhile, the *Lancashire Daily Post* said, 'The England captain has never played up to his repute this season, but he is not peculiar in that.'

The decline of the captain had been offset by the emergence of several talented local men. Arthur Cowell had partnered Crompton for England. Wing-halves Albert Walmsley and Billy Bradshaw were as fine a pair as any in football. 'Pinky' Latheron had come from north-east junior football to become a complete inside-forward. A Scot, Wattie Aitkenhead, had proved the sort of ideal utility clubs covet, but it had been the signing during the season of the great Jocky Simpson that had convinced everyone that this was a team of potential. A legend in Scotland, he was a complete outside-right, who could devastate the opposition. After an easy start to their campaign against Southend, Rovers appeared to have squandered their chances when held to a draw by Tottenham. Showing scant regard for home advantage they won the replay and then beat Middlesbrough and West Ham on their opponents' soil. Consequently, they earned the right to play Bradford City in the semi-final at Bramall Lane. By some margin Rovers were now the favourites to win the trophy, particularly as Bradford had three men absent, including the perpetual thorn in Rovers' side, Dicky Bond.

There could be no disguising the club's desire. The team was despatched to Cleveleys for a week's training in clean, bracing sea air. Unfortunately they also contrived to make organisational errors. They elected not to return to Blackburn but leave direct to Sheffield on the morning of the game, reasoning that they were better travelling by rail than undoing their good work by an overnight stay in a smoke-filled Sheffield. This meant that the team spent the morning passing from Blackpool to Manchester where they changed to another railway authority for the last leg to Sheffield. Bradford by contrast had trained locally and had no journey, making them effectively the home side.

Blackburn: Ashcroft, Crompton, Suttie, Walmsley, Smith, Bradshaw, Simpson, Latheron, Davies, Aitkenhead, Cameron.

Bradford City: Mellors, Campbell, Taylor, Robinson, Gildea, McDonald, Logan, Spiers, O'Rourke, Devine, Thompson.

Conditions were not ideal, and a strong wind roared from one end of the field to the other. It placed the smaller, lighter Rovers at a disadvantage. Newspaper reporter 'Perseus', who knew Crompton well, said, 'He was more racked by nerves than I ever saw him in an international match.' It was later agreed that his nervousness spread, and several players were uncharacteristically affected, the desire to see Crompton in a cup final creating a burden of responsibility. The captain then found he had a fateful decision to make since he won the toss and had choice of ends. In such a situation his customary action would have been to face the wind and seek to finish the game with an advantage. Anxious to get the game out of the way, he elected to play with it.

Bradford battled the elements shrewdly. They pulled Spiers and Devine back and seldom attempted to take the initiative. In addition, they utilised the bizarre configuration of Bramall Lane to good advantage. Because it served as the Yorkshire cricket ground, one entire side had no stand. Whenever a ball was kicked out on this side it travelled a long way on to the cricket surface and much time was spent retrieving it because the hallowed turf had to be crossed carefully. The Bradford full-backs started running down the clock early and by half-time had repeatedly found the cricket ground. Even so, Rovers had three good chances, the first falling to Simpson who was normally deadly when he came in from the wing. Over-eager, he snatched at the shot and it cleared the crossbar. Twice Gildea used his hands in the penalty area. On the second occasion the linesman spotted the offence and flagged but the referee declined to consult him. Ernest Needham, the old international who was present, was not too sure about the first but was adamant that the second was a penalty.

By half-time the destiny of the tie appeared settled, and Rovers afterwards acknowledged that they realised the game was up. Even so the referee's influence had not ended. When Jimmy Ashcroft dropped to his knees in taking a cross, he was close to the dead-ball line. Before he could move, he was pushed with both hands by O'Rourke so that his momentum carried him with the ball over the line. Mr Heath awarded a corner, a decision Needham confirmed was erroneous. John Lewis, the well-known ex-referee, said that O'Rourke lifted the goalkeeper. Crompton and Ashcroft were furious, but they lost vital concentration. They defended the corner at the expense of another. When that came across Crompton had the opportunity to clear the ball, but he elected to wait for it to come down so that he could clear further and O'Rourke charged down his clearance to open the scoring. It was a rare error from Crompton who ought to have headed the ball out. Blame for Crompton could also be attributed to a second goal from Devine. He was dispossessed by O'Rourke, although it subsequently was found out that the Bradford player was offside. Thompson scored again to make the game safe. It was a crushing blow to Crompton, but he displayed little emotion.

'Still the Rovers' captain like the excellent sportsman that he is took the rebuff from fate valiantly,' said the *Lancashire Daily Post*.

He even intervened to prevent a nasty incident from developing. At the end of the game a linesman, J.P. Crook, had taken charge of the ball when he was assailed by the Bradford captain Spiers who attempted to snatch it from him. As they struggled, both men fell and, to the surprise of all, two more of Bradford's players, Thompson and Taylor, joined in the quest to wrestle the ball from the linesman. The inanity was ended by Crompton, who strode into the melee and tossed the players aside. The three players were later charged by the FA but escaped with censures after apologising. In mitigation Bradford produced a guidance from the FA ten years previously that stated that it was the duty of the winning captain to hand the ball to the referee.

Rovers' failure was overshadowed by that of Crompton. It was not the first time that Crompton had not performed well but it was the first time when he had been the culpable one when so much was at stake. 'Perseus' said of him, 'But he had no superior as a dominating player when the need was greatest, especially in international matches.' People rushed to judgement on Crompton and the consensus opinion was that he had reached the end of a long and glittering career. It was impossible to overlook the fact that his form all season had been sketchy. Age catches up with all players and big men are more prone to the slowing of their powers. The public unveiling of his frailty had come at an inopportune time with the Home International tournament on the horizon. There were clamours for him not to be selected against Scotland and it was pointed out that Crompton himself appeared to have been anticipating a termination of his England service. The demands of his newly launched motor engineering company had caused him to withdraw from the FA tour of South Africa the previous May. It had given rise to questions about Crompton's commitment or desire to serve England. Against this background Crompton still had his friends. 'Olympian', writing in the influential, *The Buff*, had no doubts:

'No finer man than Crompton has ever played the game. He has a reputation for extreme fairness and is playing as well today as when he started. It is a safe surmisal that he has more international caps to get yet.'

A week later his faith was confirmed: 'Crompton was an even greater success because his apportionment was greater. There was not a better man on the field and here he quite justified that which was written in my corner a week ago to the effect that I should be surprised if he did not prove himself the best English premier right-back. Strong and untiring was he and apart from some inaccurate kicks in the early stages of the second half I have never seen the England captain take the ball with such precise skill when awkwardly placed and bring it into play. If ever a professor of science as applied to football earned his fee was the Crompton of a week ago.'

At the time of Crompton's death, 'Perseus', who had followed his career closely, believed that it was the player's finest hour, 'In the first half of the Scottish match at Goodison Park in 1911, he appeared to hold up the whole opposition himself.'

The FA had honoured Crompton during the Home Internationals, when his record of caps exceeded that of Steve Bloomer, by asking him if he would sit for a portrait to hang alongside that of Bloomer, in the FA headquarters.

The game against Scotland was a cathartic moment for Crompton. The doubts about his ability to continue playing at the highest level were dispelled and player and club went into the close-season invigorated. Although they only finished 12th in the league, Lawrence Cotton believed that they were not far away from being a top-class team and set out to back his judgement. He brought in a rare talent, the Blackpool inside-forward Joe Clennell. He also welcomed back the Scottish centre-half George Chapman, who had spent a season back in Scotland.

At the end of the season the club embarked upon a tour of Austria and Hungary where they met up with Oldham Athletic. They started in Austria where their hosts were charming, and the team were entertained generously. In Hungary they found their hosts were far less hospitable. After an initial victory they followed up with another comfortable one over Magyor Testyakorlock. Unlike their previous opponents these men refused to accept their defeat gracefully and by the end they appeared more intent on causing injury than playing football. At the reception that followed, Crompton was in no mood for diplomacy and expressed his disapproval forcibly.

They were to find that their next opponents, Ferencváros, were even more disposed to the dark arts. When Rovers cruised into the inevitable lead, crowd and opponents became increasingly hostile. An inadequate referee allowed himself to be intimidated and crucial bad decisions against the side prompted Crompton to seek explanation from the referee. The culminating moment of madness came when Davies darted through the middle, evaded the goalkeeper and was about to tap the ball into the net when the goalkeeper struck him in the mouth, dislodging several teeth. Without any attempt to feign innocence the goalkeeper took to his heels and fled to the dressing room. The game was completed in an atmosphere of gathering hostility and at the end a large threatening crowd surrounded the dressing room. They were eventually dispersed by police with drawn sabres but not before stones were thrown and windows broken. The English press were quick to report the incident and they quoted Crompton as vowing that he would make sure that no English clubs played in the country again. Crompton denied this when interviewed back in Blackburn.

The *Blackburn Times* reported, 'Mr Robert Crompton, the captain, was rather startled when I told him of the sensational story of the so-called football riot. "It is quite true," said he, "that stones were thrown at us when we entered the conveyances, but it is incorrect to say that any of the players were struck. A window was broken, and that was the sum total of the damage. It was not what might be termed the real spectators who caused the trouble but a lot of young and irresponsible lads. The lads and not the adults caused the scene, and in the end, they were driven off by the police with drawn sabres which the officers always carry. It is untrue that I have said that I could use my influence to prevent any English team visiting Budapest for years to come. That is a terminological inexactitude. The thing appears to have been grossly exaggerated."'

Included in the touring party was a new goalkeeper, Alf Robinson, who Rovers believed was the last piece they needed to become a great side. They had misjudged the centre-forward position where Davies was reaching the end of his career and Aitkenhead was useful rather than great. Ultimately, they had to resort to playing centre-half George

Chapman as a somewhat agricultural frontman. A slow start was turned around and they steadily closed the gap on the leaders Newcastle United and Aston Villa. For exactly three months in which they played 11 unbeaten games, they took 17 points. They took over the leadership of the league in January and although they suffered a bad loss to Bolton in March they responded with nine points from five games, which gave them a lead they never surrendered. At the official reception to celebrate the championship the mayor, Alderman S. Crossley, said, 'Robert Crompton was a prince among captains and a veritable giant among right-backs.'

They had such belief that they also mounted another long cup run which included a momentous quarter-final victory over Manchester United that produced a memorable winning goal, rolled in by a grounded George Chapman. Their semi-final opponents were West Bromwich Albion, deemed substantially inferior to the Rovers. The game was uninspired and goalless. The nearest either side came to a goal was when Simpson struck the post in the first half. In the second half Robinson's contribution was limited to taking two goal kicks. The replay was again goalless, Rovers once again striking the woodwork through Bradshaw. West Brom did have the ball in the net, but it was direct from a Shearman corner and under the rules of the time that did not count. Extra time might have been expected to favour the superior fitness of Rovers but as the game wound into time added on for injury neither team had fashioned a chance. Then a superb combination move involving Shearman and Jephcott set up Pailor, who hit the ball on the turn with such power that Robinson had no hope of saving.

Twenty-two days later West Brom provided the opposition on what promised to be a momentous day. A win would clinch the league title for the first time in Rovers' history, with two games to spare. This time the Rovers rose to the occasion and won comfortably, giving Crompton his first national team medal. The celebrations were muted compared with those for an FA Cup win but the club dipped a toe in the endorsement market. Bob Middleton, speaking on behalf of the team, recommended the use of Oxo. The team added the Charity Shield, a game brought forward so that the receipts could go to the *Titanic* disaster fund. After the game Crompton remarked that footballers were always willing to aid charity.

The words had a painful consequence for the big man. Rovers visited Belfast to play the Irish international side for the same charity. A flailing elbow fractured his jaw and left him in such pain that he thought that all his teeth had been knocked out. Throughout his career, Crompton was much in demand for charity games and never turned anyone down. In 1914 his international colleague Ben Warren died. Crompton asked all the international team and anyone who had played with him to contribute to a fund for his widow and children and led the way with a donation of £20. An interesting game took place in February 1906, when the comedian George Robey took a team of his selection to Everton and beat their first team by five goals to two. His selection contained a Who's Who of the best in British football: McBride (Preston), Crompton, Burgess (Manchester City), Parry (Liverpool), Raisbeck (Liverpool), Robertson (Chelsea), Bond (Preston), Bloomer (Derby), Woodward (Tottenham), Robey, Booth (Manchester City).

Rovers continued to invest in top-class talent and brought in three quality forwards: Danny Shea, Joe

Hodkinson and Percy Dawson. Although they did not defend their title, they finished a creditable fifth and the following season were champions again. This time they were in such command that they won it with four games remaining.

Crompton's contribution was recognised by all.

'What the goals against remotely would have been but for the captain's incomparable merit cannot be estimated but it is certain the figure would not have been 42, the lowest since 1889/90,' revealed the *Blackburn Times*.

Looking for signs of Crompton's deterioration had become an annual event for journalists covering the Home International tournament. In the game in Wales, he was splendid as 'Hermes' noted in the *Lancashire Daily Post*:

'As for Crompton, still more than Hardy [the goalkeeper] was he the saviour of his side in the exciting tussle in the first half when Wales with a swirling wind behind them and a fine fervour of anticipation urging them on, bore down in tempestuous assaults which would have swept everything before them but for the magnificent strength and resolution of the great Rover. Crompton was a towering figure, a true international. Few men on the field could stand comparison.'

A month later the crucial game against Scotland produced a unanimous conclusion; Crompton remained a fixture in the England team.

Lancashire Daily Post:
'Crompton has his many detractors, but he has seldom played a finer game under gruelling conditions that he did on Saturday and on this form his international career will not stop short on.'

'Tityrus' in *Athletic News* said:
'Crompton established a record by making his 12th appearance in this match and after all these years he fought a magnificent rearguard action considering the strength of the allegiance and the weakness of his comrades. Never has he had a harder day's work and seldom has he been so strenuous and sure. The greatest tribute to Crompton's work is the attitude of the Scottish crowd towards him. How they loved him.'

The *Daily Dispatch* said:
'Crompton may be excused for thinking that he is reaching the end of his international career and I understand that, believing that this might be his last game against Scotland, he was particularly anxious it should not be a failure. Far from that it was an unqualified success for Crompton gave one of his finest exhibitions and that is saying a great deal for both his kicking and his tackling were well-nigh perfect.'

Meanwhile, the *Daily Chronicle* commented:
'The time for leaving Crompton out of the England team is not yet. He played magnificently, kicking well, and tackling with power that was amazing. Into the early part of the game the Blackburn Rovers seemed to be standing alone between the Scottish team and English defeat. Not only did he accomplish his own work, but he covered up the most of Pennington's and these were many for the Albion back never seemed able to tackle Reid successfully.'

Despite the club's second championship victory in three seasons there was the feeling in the town that the spectators (and Crompton) would have preferred to have won the cup. The following season, Bob Crompton was 36 and with a war raging in Europe it appeared obvious that 1915 would be Crompton's final attempt to obtain the cup medal that had eluded him. The draw was not difficult, an away tie to Swansea, who were in the second division of the Southern League, but it was not one that created much enthusiasm in the Ewood ranks.

Blackburn: Robinson, Crompton, Suttie, Walmsley, Smith, Bradshaw, McGhie, Aitkenhead, Orr, Latheron, Hodkinson.

Swansea: Hurst, Hewitt, Bulcock, Duery, Buck, Anderson, Reed, Brown, Benton, Gilboy, Lloyd.

Some of the Swansea players were known to east Lancashire people. Bould Harper Hurst was born in Adlington, lived in Heath Charnock and had started with Great Harwood, before arriving in Wales via Southport, Atherton, Bacup and Scunthorpe. He had once been offered terms by the Rovers but turned them down because he did not think he would receive enough opportunities. Bulcock and Reed were from Colne.

Swansea were at full strength, but Rovers' forward line had an experimental look about it with no Simpson and Dawson. Even so the game appeared to be routine and there was only minor alarm when Lloyd gave the home side a lead. Even though they were behind at half-time it was anticipated that Rovers would provide a second-half onslaught and so it proved. Wave after wave of attacks swept towards the Swansea goal and when Buck left the field early in the second half it appeared to be only a matter of time. In addition, Reed was limping, so Swansea had to cope with huge adversity. Somehow they survived, thanks to the magnificence of their full-backs but above all of Hurst who threw himself around the goal to repeatedly foil Rovers.

Finally, the moment arrived when he was surely about to surrender. A penalty was awarded and Billy Bradshaw, the most dependable of penalty takers, stepped up, to drive the ball not only high but wide. For yet another occasion in the Crompton era, nerves had aborted a cup campaign and this time everyone knew that it was the end. Crompton was about to join an honoured group of great players like Steve Bloomer and Charles Buchan, who were never destined to gain a cup winners' medal. This time the obituaries would need no revision as the *Manchester Football News* made clear in its cartoon.

81

4

Purpose, choice and consequence
that shape destiny

THE GREAT scholar Ralph Waldo Emerson said, 'There is properly no history; only biography.' The corollary of this is that history is shaped by great men – those worthy of having their lives detailed – and that if you understand the man, the understanding of history follows. Unfortunately, with great men, much is often written and repeated without all available evidence being consulted. The greater the man, often the greater the exclusion so that a biographer needs to return to prime sources and establish the detail. It is akin to taking a piece of old furniture and stripping away layers of veneer and polish to find the bare wood, to discount what is myth and discover what has been omitted.

Bob Crompton has always been regarded as the embodiment of Blackburn through and through. Born and raised in the town, a servant of Blackburn Rovers for most of his life, and if he opted for a retirement on the coast at Blackpool he even contrived, unwittingly, to return to the town to die. What has escaped notice is that his family came from Over Darwen, which has now become simply Darwen. To the outsider that would signify little. The civic authority is now Blackburn with Darwen. The towns conjoin. Only those brought up in the area would appreciate the significance. Blackburn and Darwen are separate entities, pooled by reason of geography but each insular from the other. 'Our Bob' being a 'Darrener' is as significant to the area as if he had been from Africa.

Historian Murray N. Rothbard clarified the objectives of his profession: 'The historian must be more than a chronicler, a mere lister of events. For his real task is discovering and setting forth the causal connections between events in human history, the complex chain of human purposes, choices, and consequences over time that have shaped the fate of mankind.'

A key part of the chain of events that shaped Crompton's destiny and made him a man of Blackburn rather than Darwen, and which expedited his path to football fame, can perhaps be glimpsed in a sombre little ceremony at Darwen Chapel on 22 December 1847. Elias and Betty Crompton had brought their six-month-old daughter Nancy for baptism. The family were not regular attenders of the little chapel that constituted the town's main religious building. Their other children, James and Elizabeth, had received no such blessing, but Nancy had been in poor health throughout her life and they knew that if she saw Christmas it would be her last. On New Year's Day they returned for her funeral.

The origins of the Cromptons probably lie near Shaw, Oldham, in the areas known as High Crompton, Crompton Fold and Crompton Moor. The name itself comes from the Anglo-Saxon 'crom' meaning bowed or crooked and 'ton' denoting a settlement. According to Ballard the earliest known Cromptons were Ellis, Adam and Robert de Crompton in the 13th century. The name Ellis (or Elias) has great significance with the Cromptons and was handed down with regularity. A playing colleague of Bob Crompton's was George Ellis Crompton, who came from Ramsbottom. Genealogical evidence suggests that the Crompton clan moved north-west, particularly into the Bolton area. Darwen lies south-east of Blackburn. Much of it is hill country, a target for the westerly winds which come from the Irish Sea, up the Ribble estuary and strike at the first rise they encounter. The winds drive the clouds which frequently deposit rain; it is not a place that encourages habitation, but land is finite, whereas people are infinite and the need for a living is constant.

Evidence suggests that the Crompton clan took the route across the moors from Bolton to Darwen. It was a logical place for them to settle. The population increased from 600 to 3,000 during the 18th century. Manufacturing was on the increase and cotton spinning and weaving, paper making, calico printing and coal mining soon became established. The Cromptons settled in, bringing their weaving skills and their experiences of animal husbandry that helped reduce the food budget. On 9 April 1787 Ellis Crompton, who had work as a weaver, married Mary Bradshaw. St James's in Darwen was only authorised for births and deaths at the time so the couple had to go 'big city' and make the trek to Blackburn to be married at the church of St Mary the Virgin, which is now the cathedral. A year later the couple were back in St James's for the burial of their first son, John, who had died at the age of two months. Their other children survived infancy and had in course to make the same journey to Blackburn for marriage blessings, John marrying Betty Harwood in 1818, James (Bob Crompton's great grandfather) marrying Nancy Ainsworth in 1819 and Martha marrying William Jepson in 1822. They also had other sons, Edmund and Ellis, and by the illness-riddled standards of the times, the children had proved robust.

The men all had employment as weavers, but in the early part of the 19th century life was hard. Success for a man was to lay sufficient food on his table for his family. Success for a woman was to keep them clothed, avoid the annual pregnancy to which she appeared destined and to keep her men folk out of the beer house. The lot of James and Nancy Crompton, born around the time the 19th century gave way to the 20th, was such. The family lived on Bolton Street, the main thoroughfare of the town. Each mouth was as much a burden as a boon. The couple were parents when they were 20 years old. Sarah was the first-born, quickly followed by Elias, who they had baptised at Darwen Chapel on 16 September 1821. To follow came Betsy (baptised on 27 March 1825), Mary (baptised on 16 March 1823), twins Jenny and Thomas (baptised on 24 October 1828), James – born two years later – and then the improbably named Crompton Crompton three years later. When it appeared that Nancy might have enjoyed a well-earned rest from child production, Ainsworth was born in 1838, followed by Joseph, Edward and Mary Jane (baptised 31 May 1848). The birth of the twins appears to have marked a watershed in the religious life of the family and it appears that the later family were not baptised, except for Mary Jane, who had lost her father when this event took place. He had succumbed to gangrene, following crush injuries on his leg which was trapped in a machine at work. James, who became a shoemaker, was 17 and a half before he was baptised, at Holy Trinity, not St James's.

Elias, Bob Crompton's grandfather, survived infancy, married and started his own family. James was born in 1842 and Elizabeth in 1845. Then came the brief six-month life of Nancy. It perhaps provoked a turning point in the lives of Elias and Betty. They turned their back on Darwen; both James and his father Elias were now working as dyers, and moved to Stanley Terrace in Blackburn, where Elias obtained work as a labourer. The move of his grandfather to the town that was to play a key role in the story of football can be interpreted as being pivotal in the events that led to Bob later becoming captain of England. Although at the time of Crompton's birth Darwen was as powerful a football force as Blackburn, its sporting power waned as those of its neighbour rose. Interestingly many contended that the Darwen right-back, John Ralph Leach, a contemporary, was the finest right-back in football, but his worth was never recognised because of the club's status.

Before they left for Stanley Street in Blackburn, Elizabeth gave birth to sons Robert in 1849 and Thomas in 1851. Their early years in Blackburn were dogged by misfortune. Thomas died at the age of five months and Elias's health declined and his labouring job at William Birtwistle's Stanley Street Mill became difficult. He had, though, acquired a reputation as a good, conscientious man and at the start of September 1868 he was able to obtain the tenancy of the Rose and Thistle Hotel in Greenbank from Thomas Boardman. The inn was just around the corner from Harwood Street where at number one the family made their home.

With Elias's health in serious decline the move had logic. Elizabeth was the daughter of James Jackson, a Darwen innkeeper, and knew the trade. Jackson had originally been a farmer on Sough Moor but recognised that there was a requirement for somewhere where travellers taking the difficult route from Bolton to Blackburn could partake of hospitality and converted his premises to an inn. Within a matter of days of becoming a landlord, Elias was in the magistrates' court, being fined five shillings for serving whiskey at five minutes past eight on a Sunday morning. In February 1868 he was back in court for the same offence, although, as his wife explained to the magistrates, there were mitigating circumstances. He was in poor health and his brother Crompton, who now lived in Cuerden, and Thomas, who was still in Darwen, had come to visit. The brothers and Elias's sons, James and Robert, were drinking whiskey and beer before opening hours but no sale had taken place. Surprisingly, he was fined five shillings, the magistrates stating that it was his second offence.

Elias's illness proved terminal, and he died in September 1869, aged 48. He was interred at the church of St Mary the Virgin at the heart of the town. By then James was married and had just had a young son, Robert, but he remained at home and took over as the head of the household, which included Elias's widow, Elizabeth, and Robert, his brother, who were running the hotel. Gradually Robert took charge and in September 1877 the licence was transferred to him from his mother. He had married at the start of the year and needed to get his affairs in order. His bride was Alice Utley, (sometimes spelled Uttley), daughter of Robert Utley, a man from Foulridge near Colne who had settled in the town when he married a Blackburn woman.

Utley had prospered by never being afraid to change his life. He had once had a music warehouse on Northgate, where he repaired musical instruments. In May 1866 he and another shopkeeper, Thomas Margerison, a clogger, were ejected by the landlord, the local MP Joseph Fielden. The following year he was successful in having the licence of the Albion Inn in Smithies Street transferred to him. He later became the manager of an iron foundry. Life in the licensed trade was no sinecure. On Audley Range there was the Royal Edward (Joseph Thompson), situated next door to the Rose and Thistle, the Greenbread Inn (James Thompson at number 140), the Prince of Wales (William Dawkins at number 90) and the Recreation Inn (Leonard Moulden at number 20). Licensees were tempted to cut corners to survive, which led to Crompton's appearance in the Blackburn Police Court in October 1880.

The *Blackburn Times* of 9 October 1880 reported, 'Robert Crompton, landlord of the Rose and Thistle Inn, Harwood Street, was summoned for having his house open for the sale of beer, spirits etc., at 5.45 on Monday morning. John Evans was summoned for being on licensed premises during prohibited hours. PC Dobson said that he along with PC Holden was on duty near the defendant's house on Monday morning, when they saw the defendant Evans go in and order threepenny worth of whiskey. The whiskey was supplied and paid for and witness then asked the landlady what she was doing with her house open before six o'clock. Witness told her that her husband would be reported.

'Witness, on being cross examined by Mr Radcliffe, said that Mrs Crompton told him he might go and look at her clock if he would, but he did not. Mr Radcliffe contended that Mrs. Crompton really thought that it was six o'clock and so supplied the whiskey openly. Superintendent Ward said that they sent the officers in consequence of recurring complaints, but it was from an anonymous party. The bench thought there was a doubt in the case and dismissed it. The Chairman remarked that the officers were justified in bringing the case before the magistrates.'

From the article it can be gathered that a licensee's hours were long, that local business rivals were not scrupulous about their tactics and that Crompton was sufficiently well thought-of in the business community to be given the benefit of the doubt. Why Evans, a 32-year-old stonemason from Riley Street, but originally from Radnor in Wales, wanted whiskey prior to six o'clock in the morning was not commented on.

Robert Crompton senior was a sound businessman who ran his business sensibly. When he retired, his property in Blackpool, Cornwall Villa, was a substantial residence. His estate when he died in 1914 was valued at £11,037, a fair sum for a man of his generation.

5

Player, leader, man

TO UNDERSTAND Bob Crompton, it is necessary to segregate his qualities as a player, leader and a man. Although these qualities are interlocking, they are distinct and dividing them helps unravel the complexities of the great man.

The words of one of the greatest football commentators, James Catton, are a good starting point to evaluate his playing prowess: 'A player and a half, even in an England team of great personalities.'

There is evidence that Crompton's early days gave few hints of him elevating his game to these heights. Rowland Francis, who wrote for the *Blackburn Times* under the pen name 'Ranger', had a brother, Charles, who preceded him at the paper, and had watched Crompton's career commence. In an open letter to Crompton, Rowland wrote:

'In the days of your youth, when associated with minor scratch teams, you were looked upon as a big, overgrown schoolboy, noticeable for heavy charging, a polite expression for rather rough play. Crompton was a large youth and grew into a big man. Five feet ten and a half inches was tall for the time, but he also weighed close to 14 stones, significantly heavier than most footballers. His muscular leg development was marked but there were plenty who matched him.

'What made him virtually unique was his upper body development. He had a heavily developed torso, a consequence of not only his time in the baths but a working life spent plumbing. He was by any standards a hard man and he had no qualms about using his strength, although as can be seen from his own views on full-back play, he had a considered approach to employing it. Football at the time was a hard game with bodily contact frequent and damaging. It resulted in confrontation but Crompton's control of what was a simmering temper can be seen by these illustrations.

'All footballers have not angelic tempers and an incident which happened at Ewood on Saturday might have had serious consequences for Crompton, one of the Rovers' backs. Tonks and he had a tussle which resulted in both rolling over the goal line, Crompton's weight bringing Tonks to grief. While they were on the ground, Tonks kicked at Crompton who on regaining his feet shook his fist ominously at the Wanderer. Fortunately, Crompton restrained his anger short of coming to blows. Carter and Brandon rushed up to extricate their club-mate from a dangerous situation. It is such incidents as these that begets rough play and creates bad feeling between players.'

The game with Wolverhampton took place on 18 February 1899 when Crompton was 19. The censorious tone of the article veils both the surprising maturity of the young man who made his point without incurring ejection and his confidence in his physical ability in that he was not willing to be intimidated by an older man.

Three years later in the final of the Lancashire Senior Cup against Burnley, Crompton was again on the receiving end.

'Hardy [Rovers' left-back] had a handful in Morrison and Brunton and Crompton on one occasion felt the full force of the outsider for which by his attitude he meant to give something in return,' the *Lancashire Daily Post* reported.

It was another example of what had become common knowledge; if you used rough play on Crompton, he would not turn the other cheek, but he would ensure that it was within the letter of the law.

A November 1902 criticism of his full-back partner Jack Eastham, who conceded a penalty in that game, displays Crompton's qualities of observing the rules of the game:

'This was for a deliberate trip on the part of Eastham who did one of the most foolish tricks imaginable. In addition, he placed the honours of the game at stake. It is not to a man's credit when he is fairly beaten to bring his opponent to the ground in an underhand method. When did we see Bob Crompton stoop to such a low level? The captain was in his finest form, a giant in defence and an artiste in his moves and a beautiful exponent to watch,' said the *Lancashire Daily Post*.

At the age of just 21, Crompton's play attracted his first written tribute, from the *Post*'s 'Perseus' on 6 October 1900:

'Bob Crompton is probably playing better football than ever previously if what Blackburn friends tell me is anything like correct and I am sure it must be. Perhaps admiration for the ruddy-faced back may in some small measure increase the worth of their encomiums but that apart there can be no doubt that Crompton has been in first-rate form particularly at Derby last weekend where his dashing tackling and stone-certain kicking were the object of sincere admiration. He appears to have put something on his speed since last season and has generally developed his powers. Still quite a youth his future looks bright for happily he is a good fellow as well as a good footballer. Not good in the sense that he gives himself over to excesses of jollity but in that he is a steady, thoroughly reliable fellow who can be trusted to keep himself fit and play his hardest from start to finish.'

'Perseus' was perhaps the first to comment on an aspect of Crompton that became increasingly apparent as the seasons passed: he never stopped trying to improve. Initially he had lacked the speed to cope with flying wingers, but he worked at it assiduously. Within a short period of time his speed improved, and he was able to match opposing wingers, although the ever-honest Crompton later acknowledged that he did not deserve the ovation he got from the Scottish crowd when he ran stride for stride with a flying international winger. He later disclosed that he had hold of his opponent's waistband for the entire duration of the sprint.

In his 12th game at left-back for the first team, Crompton was called upon to face the lightning-quick Charlie Athersmith at Villa Park. His introduction to the first team had been successful but nobody expected him, playing on his wrong foot and with inferior basic speed, to be able to cope with his opponent. Jack Hunter took him on one side and gave him advice that he was to remember all his life:

'Hang on to Athersmith. Don't give him an inch of room. Get the ball or the man but do it fairly. If he has a yard start you will never catch him.'

Although Rovers lost, Athersmith did not contribute to the defeat and Crompton had commenced a technique that he honed to perfection as witnessed when he played for England.

The *Lancashire Daily Post* wrote, 'The famous international [Crompton] was pitted against a sprinter who was much too fast for him. That fact though did not disconcert him. He watched and waited. He so manoeuvred that he seemed always to be in the right place at the right time. The forward whose speed was his chief asset was thrown off his game simply because Crompton appeared to be ever in the way of the ball. That was the point to which the international devoted his attentions. If he could intercept the ball before it reached the wing his opponent's fleetness did not worry him.'

By 1906 Crompton's rise to footballing perfection can be gathered by this report in the *Post*:

'The finest player on the field was Crompton whose work was faultless. No matter whether tackling, feeding, or clearing he was always excellent. His magnificent exhibition was due to his co-ordinating perfectly his master mind to his master feet.'

Crompton's views on the role of a full-back in football are recorded in October 1908 in the *Blackburn Times*, under the headline 'The Full-Back Game':

It is difficult at this time of day to say anything new on the subject of back-play in association football. The qualities of a back are exactly the same as those which were indispensable at the very beginning of English football, but there may be some little interest in considering the manner in which they are applied nowadays. Essential qualities for a good back are height, strength, speed, and weight. I am no believer in the little player in any portion of the field.

There have been a host of clever little men in the history of the game who have received, and worthily the highest honours open to a footballer. But how much better a player would each of these men have been for an added inch or two in stature! In those old days, when forwards relied to a great extent upon their dribbling powers, it is possible that a small man by reason of their superior quickness and the difficulty there would be in charging them effectively, deserved to be encouraged; but today, when mere cleverness, in England at any rate, is at a discount and the teams depend upon quick, sharp dashes into goal, ending with a fast shot or a 'header' between the posts, heavy men and tall men are the most deadly.

The Qualities of a Good Back

To meet these rushes, then, a back should be able to stand up to a vigorous wing, to head out, no matter how fast the ball may be travelling, to be speedy in case he has to race for the ball, and above all – and especially if he not be fast – to be smart in recovering from an abortive tackle, so that he may run back and re-gain a defensive position. When I say 'stand up' I do not mean that a back should 'stand to be shot at' by active opponents. There is no better method of defence than a vigorous attack and when his goal is threatened the back's play is to get in the first blow. Under no circumstances should he allow himself to be forced back into goal; rather should he dash out to the ball when the odds are ten to one against him than hamper his own goalkeeper and allow the enemy to get in a shot for which he is 'unsighted'. When play is in midfield, too, the aggressive policy is the best, provided that your partner can be trusted, although of course, the alteration of the offside law, which allows forwards to stand on the half-way line, prescribes caution in 'following up'.

The Art of Defence

The usual method of defence, and the one which I believe in, is for the back to pay particularly attention to the outside-forward while the half-back in front of him watches the inside-forward. The other back at the moment at which any one of his colleagues tackles runs into centre, to cover a possible slip or to intercept a pass, while the other two halves hold the opposite wing in check. There are people who argue that a more effective disposition would be for the backs to cover the inside men and the half-backs to hanger on the outside-forwards; but experiments made by my own team have proved that to be a fallacy. Inside men always lie nearer their half-backs than wingers, and if a full-back lies on an inside player he must necessarily very often find himself further up the field than his own half and with the flank consequently turned.

It may be said that a back need not lie right up when his half-back is tackling an outsider but what good would he be at all if he is not near enough to prevent the winger's partner taking a pass and settling on the ball? On the other hand, with the half-back waiting on the outside player he can prevent the man passing either out to the wing or to the centre; or, if he fails in this, the full-back can cover him in either direction.

My Model Back

If I ever had a model for back play, I think it would have been Tom Brandon, the old Blackburn Rovers and Sheffield

Wednesday international. He was, in his best days, a very dashing player, a wonderfully sure kick and a great tackler. His rushes seemed risky, but he seldom failed to get either man or ball – or both. In his later years he lost some of his intrepidity and developed a habit of falling back into goal. I have been accused of the same thing myself on occasions, but I venture to hope that it has been without real reason. It has usually occurred when I have been beaten by the outside-forward and when surely it was better for me to make the best of my way into goal rather than enter upon a vain pursuit of my antagonist.

And this brings me to the complete understanding which ought always to exist between a back and his goalkeeper. There have been many instances of almost perfect defences, due not so much to any outstanding ability on the part of either backs or goalkeepers as to the three working smoothly together, just as there have been many cases of matches being lost through confusion at the critical moment among the rear guard. I not only believe in the back who keeps well out under pressure, but I believe in the goalkeeper who makes him go out and is not afraid to open his mouth when he is prepared to take the ball himself. Nothing looks worse than to see a custodian and a back falling over each other to get at the ball. The blame in such a case must fall on the goalkeeper, for he always has the advantage of being able to use his hands, and a simple shout of 'All right!' would enable the back to face round and keep the onrushing forwards at bay.

Methods of Attack

It is often said that the defence is stronger than the attack in football today, and that something is required to enable that more goals be scored in order to maintain public interest. Personally, I think that last season produced quite sufficient goals for the forward play we got, and I am convinced that the laws as they stand afford plenty of scope for more scoring if the forwards really understood the game. The new offside law is not taken advantage of as it ought to be to spread eagle a defence, nor do players vary their styles in order to bewilder backs as they ought. Examples of the success of the long passing game will recur to every follower of football, but how often do we rap forward lines who deliberately adopt and keep up such a style. Very seldom indeed as I have had occasion to lament when captaining a team, and to congratulate myself upon when opposing doughty rivals. The short-passing game is all very well in its way, but every back knows how to meet it. No defender in the world, however, can keep up for long under the pressure of an attack by men who cross the ball from one wing to the other and avoid the conventional custom of forwards centring. But when forwards stick to one style, even though they are sent back time after time, the backs have an easy task.

A Personal Instance

I may be excused for mentioning a particular instance of this which came within my own experience in the last England v Scotland match. The Scottish selectors placed on the left wing the famous Quinn of Celtic, famous that is as a centre-forward. The idea, I suppose, was that he would be able to utilise the trickiness and speed he showed at centre, but as a matter of fact his only idea of getting forward was to shove the ball past me and run for it and nothing is easier than to defend such tactics. There are, of course,

famous wing players who have quite stereotyped methods
which sometimes 'come off' and at other times signally fail.
Let me give a hint to wing-forwards who believe that they
must not part with the ball until the back has tackled them.
Nothing annoys a full-back so much as having been drawn
out to the wing only to see the forward centre or part before
he can get there. It not only causes him useless exertion, but
it makes him look soft. The forward who thinks because he
has once beaten a back with the ball, he can do it again and
again, will soon discover his mistake. I remember last year
a very 'smart' outside-forward who got the better once of
Sharp, the splendid Woolwich Arsenal back who played for
Scotland. He tried time after time to repeat the trick, but
every time Sharp was too good for him, the result being that
the wing was an abject failure on the day's play. A forward
who cannot impart variety to his play is not worth his place.

The Use of Weight

The most serious handicap under which a fast and weighty
back suffers nowadays is the uncertainty as to how the
referee will regard charging. The law says that charging
is permissible 'when not violent' or dangerous – which
seems like taking back with one hand what is given by
the other. The Football Association have since directed
that proper charging should be encouraged, but we still
find referees who bring undeserved opprobrium upon backs
guilty of using their weight. It is an athletic game which is
something more than an exhibition of technical cleverness,
these gentlemen seem out of place. If a forward is allowed
to use to the full an advantage he may possess in the way
of great speed, why should not the back be allowed to use
his avoirdupois to counteract it? And how in the world is a

man to charge another effectively unless he uses both his weight and speed?

More hustling of an opponent is all very well when you are close enough to rub shoulders, but how can one stop to regulate his pace to a nicety if he is making a 20 yards sprint to 'get there'? A half-hearted charge is worse than no charge at all for your opponent will then knock you down! My advice, in spite of these timid officials, is to charge whenever you are certain that it is necessary either to get the ball or prevent an opponent from getting it. If you miss the ball, don't miss the man, if by upsetting him you can reap a legitimate advantage.

Finally, no back, and no pair of backs, however good, can hope to set up a successful defence without a perfect understanding with the half-back line. This is even more important than combination in front, for without good backing up a forward line gets no chance to score goals. A settled plan from centre-forward to goal is a good thing; a complete working understanding with the rear is absolutely indispensable.

* * *

The prototype full-back of the day was governed by the tactics of the time. The paramount requirements were kicking and tackling ability. These qualities were more often found, but not exclusively, in big, strong men. The next necessity arose from the system that was being used. The full-backs played wide with the objective of nullifying the opposing wingman. The half-backs formed a block across the inner field, opposing the two inside-forwards and centre-forward. Although the wing-half might provide cover if the full-back was beaten, his priority was to shadow the opposing inside-forward. The full-back sought to pin the wingman to the touchline, at the same time cutting off the inside pass. That forced the winger to try and beat the full-back by speed or trickery. If he elected speed the full-back had to try and match him. This created the requirement for speed in a back. If he was beaten and the wing-half could not help, the responsibility for curtailment fell on the opposing full-back who moved into the middle when the attack was directed down the opposing wing. It required considerable speed for a back to come over to the opposite wing in time to make a challenge. In the meantime, the beaten full-back had to stay on his feet and move back diagonally to position himself where the other back had been. Therefore, the size and strength requirement had not to over-ride the need for pace.

'Perseus' pointed out why Crompton was so special:

'No analysis of his attributes could ignore one element in his make-up which was unique, and which illustrated perhaps more than anything else his claim to be regarded as a real footballer. He had a scorn for that resort of the lesser back, putting the ball out of play. He would scheme all the time to keep it in play, even on occasion to the point of endangering his goal as he wheeled and travelled the other way, a proceeding which he almost alone could adopt by reason of his strength, speed and two-footedness.'

Not everyone was so receptive to his unconventional approach. *The Buff*, commenting on the own goal Crompton conceded in his benefit game in 1904, commented, 'For a back of such class Crompton has a particularly bad record in this respect. One cause of this may be found in the fact that Crompton is most sportsmanlike in his play and his downfall has sometimes been brought about through endeavours to keep the ball in play instead of securing a goal kick.'

Others saw the same situation in a different light. 'Hermes' noted Crompton's penchant for own goals: 'Very few forwards have beaten Robinson as often as Bob Crompton. This is all part and parcel of his greatness. Other merely excellent full-backs would not get to the ball at all.'

Crompton's ability to throw his body at shots and block them was unequalled among contemporary defenders but it meant that occasionally he only diverted the ball past his own goalkeeper.

The Buff also clarified the position regarding the most contentious point of Crompton's game, the use of his ample weight:

'One of the points often discussed about the famous back's methods was whether he was what is called a "fair" player or was "rough". It is perhaps a nice point although not so fine as might appear. He was a big man, endowed with weight and like an even bigger man who contemporaneously played in the same position, Harry Thickett of Sheffield United, fast. So that when such fellows buffeted an opponent, he was in no doubt that something had struck him.

'But honest charging is of the very warp and woof of football although recent generations of supersensitive referees have bred a belief that it should be cut out and both Crompton and Thickett were quite fair players.

'They used the battle axe rather than the rapier but with skill, and to handicap their weight was just as absurd as it would be to limit the delicate footwork of a James, a Meredith, and a Matthews or the speed of an Athersmith and a Templeton.

'No, Crompton, a master of move, may have felled an opponent when it was the best thing to do to stop him, but I recall few occasions when it was either dangerous – the only proviso against it – or gave rise to complaints from the victims.'

John Lewis, a top-class referee, had highlighted one of the problems that Crompton had to cope with as early as 1908, when he questioned the interpretation referees were giving on the subject of charging:

'Present-day referees were altogether too prone to penalise legitimate charging. It was not right and he had never seen a charge that was necessary that could be classed as dangerous or violent play. He wanted to impress upon them that if a charge was necessary, it was an impossibility for a referee to punish a man for that charge. Some men were more speedy than others and with this advantage delivered a more heavy charge. Were they going to punish a player for being a fast runner? If so, he was punished because he possessed one of God's gifts. Were they going to punish a man like Crompton because he was of better physique than some other men? Certainly, they should act and advise all referees to think carefully what they were doing and to act honestly.'

The *Blackburn Times* stated, 'Without doubt Crompton has had more unjust penalties given against him than any other defender.'

On Boxing Day 1904 referee Thomas Kirkham, a pottery printer from Burslem, awarded two penalties for fouls by Crompton, in the space of two minutes. John Lewis, who was regarded as the best referee in the game, commented, 'Neither of those penalties ought to have been given. The charges were perfectly fair.'

The *Lancashire Evening Post* analysed the awards in depth: 'The first 12-yard kick was given for an offence which was more likely to be accidental that intentional. Crompton attempted to head the ball, in order to prevent an opponent gaining possession. In doing so he leapt slightly in the air and as he was alighting on the ground his hands lightly touched the Sunderland man. The penalty would hardly be given for jumping at an opponent and the next possible breach of the rule is pushing. Crompton confirms that he never pushed his opponent.

'Sound, impartial and careful judges are certain that in the second case Mr Kirkham was in error, Hogg dashed down the field and Crompton made way to meet his man. Then he met him with a full charge, shoulder to shoulder, sending Hogg over but at the same time using his feet to land the ball into touch. Crompton hitting the ball in this way could not have illegally used his feet and the only offence of which he could have been guilty was a stab in the back. The most surprising fact in connection with the whole matter was the promptitude with which Mr Kirkham awarded the penalty when apparently no appeal was made and he himself was a long way behind the player.'

Within the game it was known that a few individuals believed that Crompton's use of the shoulder charge was illegal and detrimental to football but his continued endorsement by the national selectors weakened their case. There are analogies to the situation of Sri Lankan Muttiah Muralitharan in cricket and the mutterings that came to a head when Darrell Hair started to no ball him because of an allegedly bent elbow. Perhaps Kirkham's decisions were random but there were many who believed that they were specifically designed to place the issue on the agenda.

More than one influential journalist raised the issue as to whether the selectors would act in the forthcoming Home International Championship and demote Crompton from the England team. In the event the selectors remained true to their principals and were loyal to their captain. What was curious was that Crompton regularly was the most penalised Blackburn defender when his full-back partners, Eastham and Cowell, were well known as men who never hesitated to trip an opponent who was too clever for them.

The great Celtic forward Jimmy Quinn made it clear how he regarded Crompton:

'As long as I live, I will never forget my international bouts with Bob Crompton. He is the best English back I ever played against. My recollections are vivid. He was a clean, virile, vigorous player.'

It should not be presumed that every opponent waxed as lyrical over battles against Crompton, and some overstepped the mark. Playing at Middlesbrough, Crompton allowed a long ball to sail into the arms of Alf Robinson when he was suddenly felled by a high boot from the winger Edmund Eyres. The studs raked over Crompton's shoulder, tearing his shirt and leaving a deep gash on his shoulder before it came to a stop against his jaw, which he had broken not long before. The Rovers players were incensed, and it appears an amazing coincidence that the target of the boot was Crompton's hardly healed jaw.

Arthur Cowell, who was closest to the action, had no doubts about the intent. When play restarted, he waited until Eyres had the ball and crudely floored him. By now it was obvious that the game was getting out of hand, but Eyres was not intimidated. When play resumed, he returned the compliment to Albert Walmsley. The referee appeared paralysed to stop the violence. He later stated that he was unable to take any action because he was unsure of the intent of the players concerned. Fortunately, there were sufficient cool heads on the field to do his job for him and the game eventually quietened down. Crompton made no complaint, although he was reduced to feeding on liquids for some time. Checks revealed severe bruising but no new break.

That Crompton retained his mastery into his last years is detailed in this report of his play on the day of his 35th birthday:

The Buff wrote, 'In the match with Bolton Wanderers the outstanding feat was surely the splendid way in which Crompton comported himself against one of the most crafty and mazy wingers in the country [Ted Vizard]. And yet it was the day on which the far-famed Robert Crompton completed his 35th year. Crompton's worths are too well-known and too well-read to make it necessary for one to enter lengthily into detail here but he is one of the very rare players, indeed I fancy he is the only player who has spent half his years in England's First Division for Crompton was 17 and a half when he made his league debut. He has now added another 17 and a half years and still stands for everything that is best in defensive play. By the close of last season Crompton had figured in 490 First Division matches besides numerous other FA Cup, Lancashire Cup, international, interleague, benefit, and even friendly matches. Ere [sic] the end of the month Crompton hopes to complete an impressive record of 500 First Division match appearances. Blessed with a fine physique, he has succeeded in taking common-sense care of that with which nature has endowed him. It is appropriate that he should captain the champion team of the land and one's wish is that he may long continue in the front rank of British backs.'

There was also an emphasis on finding a pair of full-backs who could dovetail. Even the best of backs did not always find harmony. Crompton had entered Rovers' ranks as a left-back, the foil to Tom Brandon. It placed Crompton at a disadvantage because he was right-footed and he himself commented on Brandon's penchant for falling back into goal as he played out his later games. In mentioning this Crompton was being discreet because what is unstated is that Brandon was not covering for Crompton when required to do so. When Brandon fled, Rovers endeavoured to fill the vacancy by moving Crompton to his natural flank and bringing in the inexperienced Allen Hardy. Initially he was naive, but he was a tough ex-miner and settled down to the role. Crompton aided his improvement, but Rovers' directors were not convinced and in 1901 brought in the experienced Jack Darroch, a Scot from Bury. Hardy was considerably put out and his language to the directors earned him a suspension, after which he injured himself and had to retire.

Hardy's opinions were later verified. Darroch lacked pace and a new solution was sought with the introduction of Jack Eastham, who appeared to be the soulmate for Crompton. He had been raised in the Little Harwood Inn, where his father Caleb was the licensee, so the two had been neighbours for years. On the field, though, they were diverse characters but whereas Crompton, no matter how vigorous the game, was always in control of himself, Eastham played like a force of nature, often failing to distinguish between the legal and the downright violent.

In 1904 Rovers paid the sum of £475 to St Mirren for the international full-back, Jack Cameron. He became Crompton's first real partner, tough-tackling but speedy and a student of the game. Football, though, is a contrary game, and just when Crompton's ideal partner had been found, a better one came along who was to be his foil for the remainder of his playing days. Arthur Cowell was the youngest of six children and was born in Bolton Street. The death of his father soon after his birth had forced the family to mature more rapidly than might have otherwise been the case and, after starting work as a Jacquard machinist, he knew all about the boredom and danger of the cotton mills. Given an opportunity to make the grade at football he was not going to waste it and throughout a long career that saw him capped for England he never displayed the slightest trace of nerves. Size-wise he was a complete contrast to Crompton, slight and slender, but his kicking and tackling were powerful, and his speed was allied to a considerable degree of artistry. It is doubtful whether he learned much from Crompton about full-back play since the intricacies fell naturally to him. There is compelling evidence to suggest he was completely self-taught since he was a shrewd exponent of the timely trip or little tug, which Crompton would never countenance.

Rovers' search for a suitable partner for Crompton had been mirrored in the national team where it was not until March 1907 that they found his ideal foil. For the game against Wales, England replaced the Newcastle full-back Jack Carr with Jesse Pennington, a slight, Black Country man who had worked in the steelworks. The pair were to become a legendary partnership, cited throughout the game as the perfect combination. In style

Pennington was remarkably like Cowell, although the national selectors deemed him superior, a consequence of which was that Cowell only once represented his country. It was not until after the war, with Male and Hapgood, that a pair of England backs came along who were deemed equal to Crompton and Pennington. Crompton's role was summarised by 'Perseus':

'His partnership with Pennington had passed into historic recognition but it is doing the latter no injustice to say that it is due more to his colleague's mastery than to his own powers.'

Tributes to the standing of Crompton are abundant but the great Charles Buchan perhaps summed him up in a concise manner:

'Crompton was undoubtedly the outstanding full-back of his time. A commanding personality, he was the best kicker of a ball I ever ran across.'

Crompton was generally held to be the finest striker of a ball in the game, but he seldom featured on the scoresheet. In all he scored 14 goals but nine came from the penalty spot, four from free kicks, and one from converting a rebound when his original shot was saved. Full-backs of the time were seldom spotted in the opposing penalty area. His penalty technique was simply to strike the ball hard. Undeterred when he missed, he became the regular penalty taker for three years, but the randomness of his shooting eventually resulted in him being replaced by the deadly Billy Bradshaw. From then on he only strode up to the spot when Bradshaw was absent, but never had any qualms about taking on the responsibility. It is something of a mystery why he never scored from open play because he certainly had the capacity and the desire. The closest he came was on 6 January 1900 when a thunderous shot from long range came back off the post. It would not have counted anyway as the game was abandoned after 35 minutes.

The great philosopher Peter Drucker reasoned, 'Effective leadership is not about making speeches or being liked; leadership is defined by results not attributes.' In doing so he touched on the subject of whether a man must be popular to be a great leader. John Buxton Hilton, an educationalist who later became a leading writer of detective fiction, was once appointed headmaster of an old grammar school where the previous incumbent had passed the final years of his teaching life. Standards had declined, discipline was poor, and it was an institution that was underachieving. Hilton turned around the school by leadership. He had no reservations about his own ability to provide direction but realised that in such a large organisation he needed others to follow his lead and contribute leadership.

The position of head boy had become largely ceremonial, a personal plaudit for one pupil annually, but of little practical use beyond a nice footnote on a CV. There was seldom any doubt about the recipient of the honour. Academic excellence was not a requisite, although academic competence was but the head boys were photogenic, popular and above all good all-round sportsmen. Hilton did not regard these as disadvantages, but he had paramount regard for one quality: leadership. He sought boys who saw the end picture and achieved it in a disciplined, constructive manner and in doing so influenced others to take the same path. What made Hilton virtually unique was that he earmarked his head boys in the second year, although they would not be chosen until they had finished their sixth year. In doing so he espoused the belief that leaders are born not made.

This is contrary to the opinion of most management gurus who maintain that leadership is an acquired skill and no one is born a natural leader, although they are not exactly disinterested parties. Commercial leadership courses would be reduced considerably if you start with the premise that leaders are born. It is also true that opinions on the qualities of leaders vary. One such guru used to cite the former England defender Stuart Pearce as a complete leader of men. Most serving soldiers would have reservations about being led into battle by a man who earned the nickname 'Psycho' by displays of rabid hot-headedness.

There are many parallels between the careers of two outstanding captains of Blackburn Rovers and England, Bob Crompton, and Ronnie Clayton. Both were men whom team-mates would describe as aloof. It was an aura that they carried from their teenage days when they first joined the club. Crompton, in the 25 years of his playing career, had only three friends on the playing staff: his brother-in-law Sam McClure, little-known reserve Ernest Brindle and his business partner, 'Tinker' Davies. Clayton's situation was slightly different in that he joined Blackburn at the same time as his elder brother, Ken. The brothers and their father were a tight-knit trio and the fact that the boys advanced into the first team only tightened the bond. When Ken failed to stay the course and faded from the scene, Clayton found a friend in full-back Ken Taylor. At the time, Rovers were well known for their enjoyment of life, smoking and heavy drinking was common. Taylor, like Clayton, was a teetotaller and dedicated trainer and the two often isolated themselves from proceedings to the point that it was not unknown for them not to travel with the official party. Curiously in the twilight of his life Clayton was much more gregarious and would often be found in the company of Bryan Douglas, Mick McGrath and Roy Isherwood, who in their playing days were customarily in the ranks of the socialisers.

The question that arises is whether the aloofness of Crompton and Clayton was the natural isolation of solitary men or a recognition that from an early age they expected to be leaders. Their advancement as captains came at an early age and no one ever questions that they had a natural gift for the position. There can be no doubt that a certain measure of detachment helps a captain enormously. Football teams are hot-beds of interpersonal rivalry, and the perception of neutrality is a great asset. Both men appear to have been unaware that they had the qualities that are looked for as leaders. They shared a pre-occupation with personal fitness and improvement and were models of dedication. They also looked the part, both imposing men in their carriage and comportment. When looking for a football captain it is not hard to eliminate a majority who are unsuitable but there still remains a few who look the part but put to the test are inadequate.

The *Lancashire Daily Post* of 9 April 1904 had no doubts about Crompton's qualities:

'Indisputably he is the safest and strongest back in the country and what his personality means to his comrades it is difficult to say. Captains, real captains I mean, are scarce. Bloomer if I remember rightly was the England skipper two years ago but he is not cut out for the part at all. Crompton on the other hand suits the role well. Most of all his fellows have confidence in his play, so indeed they have in Bloomer. Crompton however possesses the happy facility of being able to take in the game as a whole and of directing the operations of his men. Not only does he keep a guard on the whole game in his way, but he seems to create enthusiasm to his men.'

Both Crompton and Clayton chose to lead by example but whereas the latter remained a quiet man, once he stepped over the white line, Crompton became a voluble character.

The Buff wrote, 'Crompton, the Rovers full-back, is never so happy as when his team wins away from home. Immediately the lead has been gained you can continually hear him encourage the players and give advice to anyone who appears somewhat uncertain.'

Charles Francis of the *Blackburn Times* remarked that with his arm up raised, he was a commanding figure with a remarkable resemblance to Kaiser Wilhelm II.

'Perseus' in the *Lancashire Daily Post* said of Crompton in 1907, 'He was always a commanding figure on the field, an inspiring force and one of the few real captains in the history of the game. For strange to say, captaincy is seldom wanted, or tolerated in football. It is even frowned upon.'

Crompton became a great leader because he accepted without question all the responsibilities of the position. Dicky Bond was a right-winger for Preston and Bradford, and, to the Ewood crowd, public enemy number one. He was a born provocateur whose sly tugs and kicks were skilfully disguised from the referee if not from the spectators. In April 1910, they afforded him his customary reception but Crompton, as on field leader of the club, knew his duty.

'It is quite true that on the Saturday afternoon Bob Crompton thought it necessary to ask certain spectators on the stand to desist from guying Bond and it is a pity that these people should require a request of the full-back,' said the *Blackburn Times*.

'The Referee', writing in *The Buff*, was less inclined to blame the spectators:

'If Bond generally gets a jollying at Ewood he must shoulder some of the blame himself.'

Few questioned that even in a country where there were many fine captains, Crompton was supreme. However, there is a curious anomaly in the number of times that he captained England, 22 in his 41 appearances. The explanation is that there were still top-class players in the country who were amateurs, and the selectors would not countenance an amateur having to serve under a professional player. It was a situation in the national team that had become institutionalised due to failure to deal with the problem at an early stage. When Rovers' Jim Forrest was the only professional in the England side, he found that his status had been recognised by the organisers of the team. His ten team-mates had well-woven, comfortably fitting shirts but his was of a different, shiny material that he was only just able to squeeze into.

Crompton had become England's international captain until he had to miss the whole of the Home International tournament in 1905 because of a knee injury, sustained on 7 January in a collision with Bache of Aston Villa. He did not return until 11 March, and although he 'came back like a giant refreshed', it was too late to be considered for the Home International tournament. The following year his inclusion was a formality, but Stanley Harris of Old Westminster and Corinthians retained the captaincy for the internationals. Thereafter Crompton was the England captain unless Vivian Woodward was in the team.

It is widely quoted and true that Crompton was the first England captain to hold the position when there was an amateur in the team. The situation was created in 1907 when for the home international against Ireland, the Luton Town amateur wing-half, R.M. Hawkes, was selected for his first cap. Not even the FA could justify giving Hawkes the captaincy. It is equally true that right up to his final cap in 1914, the policy on amateur captains did not change as *The Buff*, replying to a complaint about the issue, reported:

'It has been the practice of the FA that when two men of equal ability are concerned the amateur has the advantage. I don't say these two men's abilities are equal but there is no doubt about the captain's skill or his gentlemanliness or the esteem in which he is liked by professional players throughout the country. Woodward is a man admired by everybody and I am certain that Crompton would be the last man to feel slighted because Woodward has in the instance been granted the titular captaincy. Also, I must say that the FA would be the last body in the world to act unfairly or ungentlemanly to Crompton.'

Inevitably Crompton's leadership had its critics and 'Perseus' of the *Lancashire Daily Post* later wrote:

'If he had a fault, it was that, on the basis of his experience, powers, and outlook, he was apt to direct play may be a shade too much on the field. But other players did not always act as he was entitled to expect, and it did not invariably produce the happiest results.'

There was some truth in the statement. Crompton had a fear of unknown goalkeepers, first demonstrated when Peter Platt made his debut in 1901. Platt survived the game well but was beaten by a shot for which Crompton was responsible. Instead of turning the ball to his goalkeeper, he attempted to work it clear. Wheldon stuck a foot out, made contact and it became a shot which beat Platt who was unsighted by Crompton's bulk.

In 1906 it was noted in the *Blackburn Times* that Crompton's main deficiency was that 'he is insufficiently confident in a goalkeeper'. In this case it was Billy McIvor. 'Twice on Saturday he nearly brought about the downfall of his change by attempting too daring efforts instead of leaving the ball to McIver.' The fault was never rectified. A further six years later James Crabtree was the debutant goalkeeper when it was noted that Crompton 'even imperilled his own goal once by carrying unnecessarily and unwisely away from Crabtree'.

Two years later the next debutant came along. Rovers' goalkeeper of the day was Alf Robinson, an intrepid, agile man whose bravery often passed into the vicinity of the foolhardy. His departure from the field was a frequent event and the club might have paid the penalty if Crabtree had not appeared from nowhere to hold the fort in his absence in a crucial period in the campaign for the previous year's championship. Confident in his ability to deputise, they allowed the reserve goalkeeper, Harry Langtree, to leave. They were therefore placed in a predicament when Crabtree became the first footballer to volunteer for the war and had to promote Robert Edge, son of the vicar of Blackburn, to provide cover. A product of Rossall School, Edge had gained a blue at Cambridge but had played very few games for the reserves. To Crompton he was an unknown quality and he acted accordingly:

'I am sorry to have to say that Bob Crompton practically gave both [goals] away. Bob played well in the field but whenever the Rovers goal was threatened, he would fall back between the posts in order to protect Edge and these tactics led to disaster. He hardly needed to have been so anxious about the Cambridge amateur, who shaped excellently at some different shots and was seldom at a loss,' wrote the *Lancashire Daily Post*.

The *Blackburn Times* added, 'Crompton might have given the goalkeeper more scope. He seemed anxious not to leave too much to Edge, the old Cambridge player and for that reason, once or twice placed himself and the custodian at a disadvantage. I don't think they would have scored the second goal but for this.'

Never an obdurate man, Crompton recognised his error and thereafter left Edge alone between the posts.

He never escaped his legacy of being likely to concede an own goal. In 1914 the *Blackburn Times* noted that his son 'has inherited one of the traits of his famous father. He put one past his own goalkeeper.'

The same newspaper observed in 1917, while refuting rumours of Crompton's retirement, 'Whether winning or losing, he is always the same great-hearted player and as a leader he is almost unequalled. One remembers too his chivalry to opponents as well as the strict conduct and courtesy of this fine sportsman and typical Englishman.'

If there was ever a classic example of Crompton the natural leader it came in wartime. After playing the opening game of the 1917/18 season, he made himself unavailable. He was one of only three Rovers players who were exempt from military service (engineers Chapman and Dewhurst were the others) but that pair were based away from Blackburn. Consequently, the team was normally composed of local junior players.

On 10 November they reached their lowest ebb. Away at Stoke they turned up with only nine men, borrowed two junior players from their hosts and lost 16-0. For the return meeting a week later, Crompton was entreated to come back. So were Chapman, Davies and Bradshaw, and Jack Powell, the Manchester City goalkeeper, agreed to play. In the first half it looked as if the tide had turned. With only one game under his belt in eight months, Crompton would have struggled anyway but he found that he had a doughty opponent. The veteran Stoke winger Tom Bridgett relished the opportunity for some payback against so redoubtable an adversary. 'Neither shunned an encounter and both came to earth on several occasions,' said the *Lancashire Daily Post*. When at the start of the second half Rovers fell to pieces and goals started to rain in, Crompton reacted as if he was playing in an international. The *Post* added, 'Crompton's face was a sight.' His bellows were clearly audible: 'Don't give up lads. Play your man.' The game was lost 8-1 but Crompton was still driving his men at the final whistle.

A private man is hardest to analyse and there were few more private than Crompton. Although not reticent to speak to journalists, he seldom gave an interview. It was known that he refused to contribute articles on the game or endorse products because he had principals on what he deemed to be exploiting his position. Notoriously detached in the dressing room, he was as diffident in his private life and never was at ease in the company of the unctuous. *Blackburn Times* reporter Rowland Francis commented, 'I have seen you [Crompton] shun men anxious to speak words of flattery.' His brother Charles echoed the sentiments in 1939 when celebrating the club's promotion: 'Maybe I will be mildly rebuked for writing this for Mr Crompton is a man who shuns the limelight.'

Crompton's diffidence was often misconstrued. 'Perseus', who knew him from his early years at Rovers, believed that he was the victim of self-confidence in his ability:

'This sense of mastery he was fully conscious of, and it tended to colour his contacts both on and off the field in such a way as to arouse a certain resentment at times in the minds of lesser men. And so little rifts in relationships occurred which marred the surface of his life-long association with Rovers' football. But the slow smile in which some people seemed to detect a slight touch of superciliousness was also disarming and the whole manner was only the expression of a man who knew and had studied the game from every angle.'

Crompton's funeral revealed much about the man, if only from an analysis of the absentees. Wartime was casting its shadow and travel was problematic. It is equally possible that the reporting was not comprehensive so in individual cases judgement may be precipitate. Despite all these caveats, a pattern emerges. His wife Ada had only the support of her youngest sister, Maude. Bertha McClure, Sam's widow, and their son Sam were not there. Neither were her brothers William, Fred and Thomas, and her sister, Kate Magee. The Cotton cousins, Ethel, son of Lawrence and wife of Wattie Aitkenhead, and Edith, daughter of Clemence and wife of 'Tinker' Davies, were also absent. It indicated some degree of apathy from the powerful Cotton family to Crompton, which was evident at the wedding of Davies and Ethel Cotton, when the best man was Ethel's brother, John. If one of Davies's brothers had not come from Wales it would have appeared logical that Crompton would have been the best man.

Of the great pre-war team, Arthur Cowell, Billy Bradshaw, Albert Walmsley, Percy Smith and Joe Hodkinson all lived within easy access but did not appear. Cowell had been Crompton's full-back partner and played with him for 15 years and had also served him as assistant trainer. Bradshaw had played with Crompton for 17 years and spent a year driving one of Crompton's taxis. Smith had been a playing colleague for ten years but had known him far longer. Hodkinson had been a colleague for seven or eight years. From local clubs like Preston, Bolton and Burnley, only Tommy Bamford made the effort to pay his respects. Wreaths were received from Rovers and the FA. The only other sporting organisation that troubled to honour the man similarly was Grimsby Town. Even in those troubled times one would have anticipated a less lukewarm response to the passing of a great man. To demonstrate that obstacles were not that great, William Ernest Braund, a retired headmaster and founder member and first secretary of Bristol Rovers, made the long journey from Gloucestershire despite being 75.

Yet Crompton's friends saw a different side to the man. To the Inghams, he had been a stout family prop. His wife's younger sister, Maude, was employed by him to serve in the Queen's Hotel. Her brother Fred was taken on as a motor engineer. Others also could testify to Crompton's benevolence. When Sam McClure had signed for Blackburn, Crompton found him lodgings in Audley Range, at the butcher's shop run by Thomas Hodson. Hodson's wife, Hannah, had lived in Workington prior to getting married and this helped McClure settle in the town. Later, when Hodson died prematurely, Crompton took Hannah and her son Thomas into his home at the Queen's. When Ben

Warren died prematurely it was Crompton who organised a collection for his widow among the England team. When Newton Heath awarded Bob Donaldson a benefit game in 1895, he selected the match against Rovers so that he could use Crompton's services at functions.

Some of his team-mates also had reason to be grateful for the practical benefits of having Crompton in the team. When Danny Shea, Jock Simpson and Crompton played for England against Wales at Ninian Park on a Monday the train from Cardiff arrived in Preston station at 2.25am. If Crompton had not been with them, Shea and Simpson would have been faced with some uncomfortable few hours in the waiting room until they could catch the first train to Blackburn. With Bob's resources there was one of his cars waiting to take the players home in time to get some sleep that night.

Crompton's detachment can probably be traced back to his early years. His father assumed responsibility for the family public house at the age of 20, following the premature death of his father. The consequence was that he was always mindful of the need to earn a living and there is evidence that despite the reputation of the Rose and Thistle as a sporting pub, he actively discouraged Bob from participating in sport. Further isolation came from the loss of his two closest brothers. Harry, a year older than Bob, died at the age of 13 from meningitis. Charles, two years his junior, who was serving an apprenticeship as a millwright, was 17 when he passed away. Rheumatic fever caused pericarditis and peritonitis. Infant mortality was common but having reached their teenage years it was uncommon for anyone to lose two siblings. His other brother, James, was five years older so a more remote figure than either of the two other boys and no doubt it brought on Crompton a feeling of isolation.

When Crompton joined Rovers in 1898 he found the club in a decline that intensified. The moral compasses of some of the players had contributed to that and were no example to the younger members. Tom Brandon was to leave his wife Elizabeth and son Tom (who became a footballer with Hull City) to fend for themselves in Mincing Lane when he ran off with another woman. Forced to scrape by on her earnings as a domestic servant, Elizabeth took Brandon to court to try and obtain maintenance, after which the miscreant fled to Scotland and then the USA. To exacerbate matters Brandon and another Scottish player, George Dewar, had married local sisters, so the affair had repercussions in the dressing room.

Another player, Thomas Timothy Tierney, was also in court for abandoning his family, although he pleaded domestic violence as a mitigating factor, claiming his wife had attacked him with an umbrella. At least they eventually reconciled. Ted Killean was notorious in the town for an affair with a young girl, Mary Anne Quinn, who he had no intention of marrying but passed off as his wife. That situation ultimately appeared in court with countercharges of assault. Mick Calvey was a habitual drunk who racked up a series of convictions for drunk and disorderly and was later discharged from the army as 'dissolute, incorrigible and worthless'.

Drinking was common among the players and a practice difficult to curtail. Many ran public houses. Dewar had the Swan Hotel in Astley Gate, Tierney the Eagle and Child in Chorley, George Anderson married a widow, Hannah Ainsworth, who ran the Gardeners Arms in Great Bolton

Street. In 1920 Anderson simply disappeared from the Blackpool boarding house he ran with his wife and was never seen again. Contradictory evidence suggests that being brought up in a public house had no detrimental effect on players. Among the young players who came to the club, Crompton, the Blackburn brothers Fred and Arthur, and Jack Eastham, were all raised on licensed premises. Crompton and Fred Blackburn became internationals and the other two were good professionals.

Drinking at the club had a history dating back to the early days. Before the Football League was formed the place to meet the players was the Bay Horse Hotel in Salford, where every night a group of them congregated. Others preferred to do their drinking at the Sir Charles Napier, run by Jimmy Brown's father. Fans only disapproved when the players performed badly. The committee was sometimes less tolerant, as was the case in neighbouring Darwen. In 1891 the club were elected to the Football League and, to strengthen, they brought in a couple of Scotsmen. After being the first English club to import Scottish players, they stopped the practice because Fergie Suter fled all too easily to Blackburn. Alexander and Carty came down from East Stirling and were put up at George Briggs's Britannia Inn.

The Darwen chairman, Thomas Duxbury, was already disturbed by the drinking propensities of some of his players and was not about to place his star men in temptation's way. He ordered then to secure other lodgings, the pair refused, and Duxbury reached for their cards. Unwilling to waste a good contract for a principle, the players backed down. The affair, though, was not at an end and Briggs was known to be annoyed at the incident. When the club's annual general meeting was held in the summer, Harry Holding of the Spring Vale Hotel sought a position on the committee. Duxbury spotted a conspiracy and said, 'It was drink that was stopping them from winning matches. The players were not training but remained in public houses all day.' He threatened to resign if a publican was elected to the committee. He also added, 'Carty and Alexander, the Scots who came down at the beginning of the season, had not done what they were paid for. That was due to publicans.' Less hot-tempered opinion in the town believed that there were two or three heavy drinkers at the club, but one was not Alexander, who was a lifelong teetotaller. With plenty of distractions in the dressing room, Crompton showed mature wisdom in maintaining himself aloof.

'Perseus' perhaps identified the characteristic of Crompton that resulted in him becoming a much-misunderstood figure within the club.

The *Lancashire Daily Post* said, 'He was not ungenerous in his appreciation of either his contemporaries or with the players of a later age, but a firm believer that any one of them could be made better than he was, he offered his advice in the best spirit, forgetful – if not innocent – of the truth that such help is seldom either sought or welcome.'

What is without question was that Crompton was an opponent who was respectful and magnanimous. Sir Frederick Wall once pointed out that Crompton was virtually unique in that 'he admires his foes'. Crompton once wrote of the excellence of the Scottish forward line of 1909, which contained Alex Bennett, Bobby Walker, Jimmy Quinn, Peter Somers, and Harold Paul: 'I will remember them all no matter how long I live.'

Opinions vary as to whether Crompton was unaware or uncaring of the way he dealt with advice. Yet his own dealings with the Ewood crowd are testimony to his own capacity to take umbrage. Charles Francis claimed that he had 'acute sensitiveness', a feeling that stemmed back to his early days as a teenager in the first team. *The Blackburn Times* opined, 'In the early part of his career his loyalty was sorely tested by the ill-natured attitude of a section of the home crowd, who refused to believe that the hefty youth would ever blossom into one of their most striking personalities the game has ever known.'

When Crompton sought to leave Rovers in 1901, he cited the lack of fairness of the fans as the prime reason for his desire. Throughout his long career there were always a voluble minority who would not be convinced of his merit. In 1903 he was known to be upset, when he had been absent for a few games, that there were those who did not want to see him return at the expense of Bob Haworth or Sam McClure. In his obituary the *Blackburn Times* suggested, 'It is curious to recall that even when Crompton was at the peak of his career his superlative skill was not merely questioned but frankly denied.'

In reviewing the 1908 season, Rowland Francis highlighted the strange paradox of the supreme player and his critics:

'The leading defender has been Crompton who is so consistently good and clever that his true worth is underestimated. I have heard it said by supporters, sane and responsible individuals, that the Rovers would do better without Crompton. In answer to that statement, I say that there is not a solitary club in England, Scotland, Ireland, and Wales that would not welcome him in their fold with open arms. Had it not been for his magnificent and valiant play the Rovers would have gone into the Second Division long ago.'

In 1910 when Crompton approached his second benefit, the strange barometer of his popularity had become countrywide knowledge and Blackburn's attitude to their most famous son was spotlighted. The local journalists closed ranks.

The Buff reported, 'Blackburn people were accused the other day by a metropolitan critic of being blind to the superlative merits of the team's captain and of carrying that to such an extent as to wilfully boycott Bob's first benefit five years ago. This is the veriest rubbish. Crompton got £300 then which was not a bad sum as benefits went in those days and he would not have got so much if people had stayed away. There are I fear a few old-stagers who think that a second benefit is more than any player ought to have and there are still those ultra-critical spectators who wonder why Crompton is so famous, but the great bulk of the Rovers crowd recognise the worth of their gallant back not only as the best player in his position but as a sportsman who plays real football.

'Personally, I know perhaps better than anybody his ideas and theories which govern Bob's football and I rejoice that in him Blackburn and England continue to know not only an exponent of physical prowess but a really intelligent thinking professional. It is rather a pity that the benefit occurs at a period when the team is wandering in the wilderness with little to fight for and nothing to encourage them, for I make no doubt that but for the Newcastle fiasco the gate today would have exceeded the £500 guaranteed. Crompton has again been chosen for international honours and next season if not this he may beat Steve Bloomer's record in caps, all being well.'

Crompton's first benefit match had been against Bury on 31 December 1904 and was witnessed by 14,000 fans, which was an average gate at the time. At the time *The Buff* gave no indication of any disappointment with the gate:

'Bob Crompton has every reason to feel satisfied with his recent benefit from a financial standpoint.'

In all Crompton had three benefits, all of which were well if not outstandingly supported. The takings for his benefit match against Nottingham Forest on 12 March 1910 fell short of the £500 minimum, and Rovers had to step in to make the sum up.

The problematic relationship of the crowd with Crompton was never changed as this report at the start of the 1919/20 season indicates:

The *Blackburn Times* wrote, 'I daresay if I know him at all that nobody was more delighted on Saturday over the success of Richard Walmsley, the strapping young back who is apparently destined to follow his footsteps part of the way at all events, than was Bob Crompton. The man who has been incomparably the greatest back of his generation if not of all time is well aware that the sands of his active football career are fast running out and that in the natural order of things, he cannot hope to go on much longer so that as his heart is in the team that he has led so honourably for so many years he is not likely to resent the introduction of a worthy successor. Therefore, one would have liked him to pass into the shade of football life with the general and heralded consideration to which his unique service entitles him. Instead of which, on the occasion of the last public practice match he was counted out by some of the spectators as he was temporarily stopped by a slight injury. This may have been only the feeble humour of a few irresponsible spectators but at the same time it was rather thoughtless in the case of one who has broken all records for length of play associated with one club. Whether he will return to the side or not the Rovers club and football generally are under an obligation to Crompton that can never be fully paid.'

'Perseus' noted, 'He was not always one who had honour in his own country. Some of his sharpest critics were in Blackburn itself.'

The rest of the world clearly had other views as the second president of FIFA, Blackburn shareholder Daniel Burley Woolfall, testified. In 1911 he took the floor at the club's AGM to say of Crompton that his name was known wherever football was played. Woolfall had been in Dresden a few days before and overheard the president of Dresdner SC singing the praises of Crompton and speaking of his sterling worth.

Football fans are perverse, and it is highly possible that the alienation of some of the crowd arose when the news was received that Crompton had acquired a motor car. Just as crowds today are losing their empathy with players because of their huge earnings, it was felt that a player was getting a 'bit above himself' to be motoring. There were a few cars around and the fans had no problem with the sight of ex-Rovers Fred Birtwistle driving a Mercedes and Arthur Birtwistle a Daimler. The difference was that they had always been 'gentry', the sons of mill owners, and the town was conditioned to accept their opulence of the upper class. Crompton was from the working class and the visibility of his rise did not endear him to some. Blackburn is an insular town and there had been considerable comment when Tom

Brandon acquired, and employed on the streets, a top-of-the-range racing bicycle, particularly from those pedestrians imperilled by Brandon's head down, feet pedalling furiously style of riding.

The opulent motor car blended well with Crompton's imperious bearing. Rowland Francis wrote, 'When you hold up your hand and shout advice you always remind me of one of the most characteristic attitudes of his Highness the Emperor William.' It was an unhappy combination to some people who believed that Crompton 'thought he was gentry'. In fact, Crompton utilised the car like he had his motorcycle, enjoying journeys in the Lancashire countryside. He never sought admission to the local automobile club, whose members were exclusively the town's elite, nor was he ever seen at the hill climbs organised so that car drivers could show off the merits of their machines.

One local man who was less inclined to be judgemental over Crompton's mechanised mobility was John Duckworth, a carter from Intack. On 7 August 1910 he was driving a two-horse lorry when he stopped at the Queen's Hotel to take a drink. The horses set off at the gallop and Duckworth, chasing after them, grabbed the front of the lorry but then slipped and was run over. The horses were eventually stopped a quarter of a mile away by Henry Ashcroft and John Thomas Parker. Duckworth received severe lacerations to his head and the horse ambulance was called. Realising that it might be too late, Crompton got his car and ran Duckworth to the hospital.

He was a fair cricketer, batting at number six and bowling at a brisk pace. After his youth he never played regularly but sometimes turned out for Rovers in charity games when work permitted. He once took 5-19 playing for Rovers against East Lancashire. As befits a publican he was also as handy with a billiards cue as anyone at the club, save Tom Booth who was sufficiently skilled to play in the English Amateur Championship. He was, though, as sparing in his billiards as he was in his cricket.

FOOTBALL CARICATURE.

ROBERT CROMPTON AS A MOTORIST.

DRAWN BY C. L. ENGLAND.

6

When the playing had to stop

THE ANNOUNCEMENT that the Football League would recommence in August 1919 caught most clubs unprepared. The finals weeks of wartime football were spent in efforts to evaluate returning players and discover new talent, sometimes to replace the first category. Rovers discovered that few of their once great team were not willing to return and have another fling at glory, although the fallen Eddie Latheron was an obvious loss that could not be camouflaged. Alf Robinson, Arthur Cowell, Albert Walmsley, Percy Smith, Billy Bradshaw, Percy Dawson, Joe Hodkinson, Johnny Orr and Alec McGhie all reported, as did the oldest of them all, Bob Crompton.

For some the failing of the flesh was too great. Wattie Aitkenhead attempted to return but his doctor vetoed his resuming. Another Scot, the great Jocky Simpson, was also found to be in a weakened state. Rovers booked him into a health spa at Harrogate for a 16-day course of treatment, but Simpson fled after a day, unable to bear the place, and refused to return even when the club offered to foot the bill for his wife in a Harrogate hotel.

Crompton had spent the initial four months of 1919 turning out a little more often, managing five games, and when Rovers reported back for training he appeared to have no reservations about his ability to resume. Close friends voiced their concern, one saying:

'Bob Crompton's friends are urging him to retire while he is still at the zenith of his fame, instead of going down into a discreditable old age like so many other great figures in sport.'

The words appeared to have little influence. He played in both the public practice games, without comment about ageing making him inadequate for postwar football. On the eve of the season the *Blackburn Times* gave no indication that Crompton was struggling:

'Veteran though he is Crompton will again captain the side which he has led with such distinction and with which he has been actively associated of 23 years. Though he may have lost some of his pace he still retains the sound skill and judgement which have made him famous in league football and in internationals and continental circles. His mere presence in a team is a great stimulus to the other players who have undoubted confidence in his ability and are ever ready to perform to his capable leadership.'

On 30 August Rovers opened the season at home to Preston. The public were unaware of the situation with Crompton until they saw Percy Smith lead the side out, with Dick Walmsley, who was about to be discharged from the Border Regiment, at right-back. Afterwards the news leaked out that Crompton did not consider himself match fit and would not return until he was satisfied; he would not be a weakness. As Rovers won by four goals and Walmsley displayed amazing speed for a full-back, it became accepted that Crompton would fade from the scene.

Just over a week later, on a Monday at Preston North End, Crompton made his anticipated return. After 15 minutes he left the game with a sprained knee and apparently disappeared from the club. It was, though, in some respects the least of Rovers' worries. Few of his fellow veterans had returned capable of survival in the First Division and it was discovered that far too little attention had been paid to succession planning. Even promising youngsters like Walmsley struggled amid the mediocrity and the club had to embark on a desperate policy of bringing in whatever recruits they could find that were better than the incumbents.

Towards the end of November, Rovers signed a man who effectively put an end to Crompton having a role to play with the club. David Rollo was an Irish international, well thought-of because of his displays in the home internationals and a confident type who settled in immediately. Before the year ended the chances of Crompton ever wearing the colours again had faded from everyone's minds, particularly as he had not even returned with the reserves. On 14 February the Ewood fans were surprised to see Crompton lead the reserves out against Liverpool. The team which lined up – Bairstow, Crompton, Clough, Ross, Lowe, Dixon, Faulkner, Byrom, Eddleston, Holland and McGhie – told its own story of the state of the club. Keighley's Bairstow, Ross from Barrow near Clitheroe, Lowe from Castle Douglas on the Isle of Man, and Dixon from Leith, were all having one-match trials. Clough was a young, local left-back, so Crompton could not have had a more difficult return to active duty. He coped well. Two days later he was back on the field with the reserves at Bury. Whatever logic inspired Rovers' directors to select him for the first team, his third game in eight days, after a prolonged absence, is hard to follow but, when the team took the field at Bradford on 23 February, Crompton was at right-back. Rollo had been moved to the right wing, where a rotation policy had been in place in an effort to find a replacement for the much-missed Simpson. Despite his undoubted speed, Rollo proved that he was not a right-winger. The opinions on Crompton were more positive.

'If not so fast as he used to be Crompton lasted the game well and in his kicking and his tackling achieved a fair degree of success,' wrote the *Lancashire Daily Post*, which added that the team, though, was hopeless and unresponsive to leadership:

'In spite of Crompton's repeated shouts of direction, the visitors rarely opened out play.'

At the age of 40 years and 150 days Crompton finally bowed out of active football with a sound enough performance. He might have been retained but it was obvious that Rollo needed to return to his natural position and the directors finally heeded Crompton's advice on the right-wing position. He had maintained that Robert Faulkner, a Scot who had arrived in August, was the best man for the position, believing him to be the best crosser of a ball he had seen at the club, apart from the great Simpson and possibly Billy Garbutt. He was permitted a run of consecutive games.

By winning seven of their last ten matches, Rovers escaped relegation and were permitted to embark on team rebuilding. In May Crompton signified that he would not play again, stating that it was time for younger men.

His decision was followed by Bradshaw (17 years' service), Albert Walmsley (12 years) and Percy Smith (ten years). With Crompton's 25 years of active service Rovers lost a staggering 64 years of experience.

Crompton got on with his life. He had enough business interests to look after and had no need to involve himself further. There were plenty of businessmen in the town who believed they had a role to play at the club but, although the team was stabilised, the boardroom was in a state of change. Lawrence Cotton, who had been succeeded as chairman by his brother Clemence, had died, creating a vacancy. Lawrence had always been the most driven of the brothers and Clemence was not really interested in continuing without him. It became known that he would stand down at the annual general meeting in June, although he was willing to continue to act as a director. Back at the AGM in June 1911 Lawrence had stated that when Crompton retired from playing, he would be nominated to become a director of the club. Even though he was no longer alive to do this personally there were sufficient shareholders of the same view.

Crompton's business acumen was undeniable, and his presence would bring repute to the board. He was sounded out and took the hint sufficiently to apply to the FA for permission to put himself forward for membership, which all ex-professionals were forced to do. That was a formality and, on 22 June 1921, Crompton attended the AGM at the Co-operative Hall, having been nominated for election. Five directors normally retired annually and faced re-election, but the number was reduced to four because of the death of Lawrence Cotton. The retiring directors were John Eddleston, Harry Garstang, J.W. Walsh and John

Cotton. Proposed with Crompton were J.H. Chadburn and Thomas Harris. Crompton's election appeared a formality, but the voting reflected the interests of the shareholders and not public opinion.

Eddleston polled 289, Garstang 268, Crompton 266, Walsh 240, Cotton 197, Chadburn 170 and Harris 50.

Among the shareholders there were many unknown alliances. There was also more than one director who considered that Crompton had treated him with disdain. On the other hand, the club had ex-players already on the board, in the personage of Johnny Forbes, Jimmy Forrest, Harry Garstang and Dick Birtwistle, who probably understood Crompton better. If there were those who thought that Crompton might step in to play a key role in team affairs, they were soon disillusioned by the leaked news from the board that he would have no greater say than Forbes, Forrest, Birtwistle and W.H. Grimshaw. The first three had considerable experience of league football. The expertise of Grimshaw, a chemist and respected businessman, who oversaw the town's sanitation, is harder to explain.

Rovers had functioned most successfully when Lawrence Cotton had assumed an autocratic role and utilised an efficient secretary, Bob Middleton, to achieve his aims. When Cotton died the leadership was lost and neither Clemence Cotton, nor his successor, J.W. Walsh, believed they could provide it. Taking their lead from progressive clubs they decided to appoint a full-time professional secretary-manager. In February 1922 they selected the old Newcastle United player, Jack Carr, for the role. Carr had the credentials. Not only had he played twice for England, but he had also experienced club success and had three championship medals as well as appearing in three FA Cup finals, where he was once on the winning side. When his playing days were over, he immediately made his future career direction known by becoming assistant trainer at Newcastle.

Despite being backed by the board in bringing in new men Rovers finished 14th, 8th, 16th and 12th, which made them an average side. Carr did lead them to the FA Cup semi-final in 1925 but they were unexpectedly beaten by Cardiff. It was not a woeful record but FA Cup defeats at the hands of South Shields and Corinthians were embarrassing. In December 1926, under pressure from the board, Carr resigned. The board concluded that the experiment of hiring a manager had failed and they decided to revert to running operations at board level.

Informed pundits did not attribute the blame to Carr. The *Lancashire Daily Post* noted:

'The troubles which have perplexed the Rovers since the war culminate from a strange policy in the part of the management. The more mature supporters especially are finding it difficult to maintain when there is the continued bogey of relegation facing the club.'

Clearly the board needed to have someone empowered to act on day-to-day management without convening a directors' meeting. The obvious candidate for the job was Crompton, who had been earmarked for the role by Lawrence Cotton at the AGM in 1911. After some discussion he was named as honorary manager and commenced his duties at the start of January. Only his love of Rovers could have induced Crompton to take the position. He had acquired a directorship in a building firm, in which he was involved from day to day, as well as his motor business. He made it clear that he would supervise the training of the players but was unwilling to undertake the administrative duties of secretary, for which the assistant secretary, Arthur Barritt, was promoted.

Within a month it was noted that the team was performing better and that players had clearly been told to follow a pattern and not their personal inclinations. The defence had been tightened and 'where grace and safety have come in conflict, the former has been pruned', according to the *Blackburn Times*. The attack had been less obviously altered, but, according to the *Times*, 'The needs of the attack have been carefully considered and while no drastic change has been made, expertise, skill, zest and marksmanship have been grafted and a plan of campaign fashioned.'

Tragedy had struck Crompton once more at the start of the season. In September his eldest son, Harry, who worked for his father as a car salesman, took his own life by coal gas poisoning. He was just 25 years old. Before the war he had appeared likely to emulate Crompton as a sportsman. He had appeared for the Parish Higher Grade School in the final of the Blackburn Schoolboys' Cup in 1914, where they lost to Christ Church. Younger than most of his team-mates, he played at outside-left. His cousin Robert, a larger boy and member of the town team, played at full-back. The pair were photographed in the *Blackburn Times* either side of the tiny goalkeeper, Edward Coar. Even though the photograph is blurred the resemblance of the youngster to his father is remarkable. Ill health struck Harry at the age of 19 when he contracted pneumonia. Despite medical attention he developed severe rheumatism which eventually crippled him so much that he was unable to work. On the fatal day, his sister Alice had left him alone in the house in Shear Brow and when she returned two hours later she found that he had turned on all the taps on the gas oven. Harry had as a youngster also displayed a talent for swimming. In 1914 he was among those youngsters granted a free season ticket for Freckleton Street baths after proving they could swim half a mile.

His cousin, Robert Crompton, moved to centre-half and on 20 January 1917 played for the Blackburn schoolboys against Barrow. He also played at right-back when the Higher Grade School won the Blackburn Schoolboys' Cup. By 1927 it was the youngest son, Wilfred, also a winger, who was the family's rising sportsman. With his formative football years less disrupted by the war, he was in his school side that won the Harry Boyle Cup in 1921. He then played for Corinthians when they won the Ernest Hamer Cup in 1926. A year later Rovers asked him to play with their junior sides. Four days after his brother's interment in Blackburn Cemetery, Wilf made his reserve debut against Huddersfield. The *Northern Daily Telegraph* reported, 'He was not unduly prominent and comment as to his capabilities must be left to further accounts.'

Father and son coped well with their loss. By November Wilf was offered and signed professional terms. Bob Crompton oversaw every training session and brought in additional training equipment to bring a more scientific approach to fitness. In the same month it was noted in the press, 'It is a question if there is a better trained and fitter team in the league. For this result Bob Crompton is mainly responsible.'

The season brought tangible reward with a campaign that took Rovers to their first FA Cup final for 37 years after a dramatic run in which they frequently appeared to be on their way out. Their final opponents were Huddersfield Town, considered by many to be the finest team in football. They had the honours to confirm this having won the FA Cup in 1922 and the First Division in 1924, 1925 and 1926. In every department save goal, they had better players than Rovers and most considered the final a formality.

What has never been disclosed is Crompton's role in preparing Rovers for the challenge. Managers often try to convince underdog sides that they have nothing to lose so they can enter the game in a relaxed mood. Crompton believed that by conceding they were underdogs he would acknowledge that his side was inferior and was not prepared to do so. He contended that there was much less between the sides than popular opinion made out. In the semi-final Rovers had beaten a rampant Arsenal side by virtue of an opportunist goal from Jack Roscamp and finding the man for the occasion in Jock Crawford, who was supreme in goal. Subsequently the press had labelled Rovers as fortunate. Crompton instructed the players to take no account of the reports, stressing that the team had defended with great skill and utilised their strengths to obtain the result. He inferred that a biased southern press had a vested interest in Arsenal and there was no evidence during the game that they had been the superior side. He also pointed back to an incident in the quarter-final against West Ham. A penalty was awarded to the Hammers and Ruffell's shot struck the post. He was then allowed, against the rules, to seize the rebound and fire it at goal, disaster only being averted by Crawford turning the ball for a corner. This blatantly incorrect decision was used by Crompton to enhance the club's siege mentality. He also convinced them that they were fitter than any team in football and that Wembley's well-known leg-sapping turf would have no effect on them.

He knew, though, that psychology would not be enough and had to deal with the problem of the great Alec Jackson, on Huddersfield's right wing. Jackson was perhaps the finest player in the game, fast, full of tricks and a strong man. He was certainly the best man in the game for demoralising the opposition and his mastery of one side of the field was often so great that winning became a formality for the Yorkshiremen. Facing him would be Herbert Jones, a fine international left-back but a man who had no plan B in his make-up. He was lithe and athletic but he could be dominated. Years later, playing for Fleetwood in the Lancashire Junior Cup Final, he contributed in large measure to his side's dismal performance because he was completely unable to handle the South Liverpool winger, Alan Hughes. Crompton took Jones to one side and carefully deconstructed Jackson's play, making technical suggestions on how to cope with him. He also had special instructions for the young left-half, Aussie Campbell. It was Campbell who was to be given the key role. Crompton wanted him to always be within reach of Jackson if he beat Jones but also wanted him to cut off Jackson's supply by sticking close to the vastly experienced Bob Kelly and not giving him time to thread passes out to the wing. Crompton's part in these crucial technical adjustments has never been disclosed.

Part of Crompton's desire was that Rovers played with a high tempo from the start, not giving the Yorkshiremen a chance to settle. Even Crompton could not have scripted the events of the first minute. Rovers obtained a throw in front of the Royal Box. Puddefoot and Thornewell worked the ball up the field and found Roscamp, whose route to goal was blocked by Barkas. Unusually Roscamp attempted the delicate and chipped it over him. Unsurprisingly his touch was heavy, and the ball sailed towards Mercer in the Huddersfield goal. It was a routine catch but for the fact that Roscamp was clearly fired up. Mercer did indeed take the ball, but he fatally froze and was immobile on the line when Roscamp dipped his shoulder and charged him. The collision was violent enough to leave Roscamp's upper arm a mass of bruises, but it was worse for Mercer who lost the ball, which spilled over the line as he fell.

As play progressed it became evident that Rovers' preparations for the game had been almost perfect. Tommy McLean scored a second goal, but it was the performances of Jones and particularly of Campbell that dictated the game. Having a consistent genius like Jackson in the side can have its drawbacks and it took Huddersfield some time to adjust to the fact that he was not producing. It was said after the game that 'Jackson has never played so badly' but it took the half-time break for them to find a solution. When they returned, he had moved to inside-right and he did reduce the arrears, but Campbell was magnificent and allowed him no other chance. By the time Roscamp clinched the game, five minutes from the end, it had to be acknowledged that Rovers had won because they were better prepared and superior. How much of this was due to Crompton? One player who knew him well, Joe Clennell, a team-mate in the 1912 championship-winning side, had no doubts. Years later he revealed Crompton's beliefs:

'Goalkeeper and backs were enough in the penalty area. If the inside-forwards thought of dropping back, he would get blazing mad. "Keep going forward" was his motto and it provided the finest team I ever saw. A team where you knew what every other man was going to do and where to find him.'

It was also confirmation that the primary inspiration behind the championship wins in 1912 and 1914 was Crompton.

Crompton made no effort to take any credit for the cup victory, giving no interviews or being present on team photographs on the day. When they returned to Blackburn and toured the town in an open-top coach, however, he was afforded pride of place alongside Healless and the cup, although with the chairman J.W. Walsh at his elbow. Later when the team was photographed back at Ewood he was included in the group but so were two other directors, John Eddleston and John Chatburn. Crompton made no effort to take the credit for team tactics or give an interview of any kind. Equally the tributes for his part in the proceedings went unacclaimed. Most of the directors and civic dignitaries rose to speak at the celebrations but all chose to ignore Crompton. Crompton made no effort to speak to the press and the closest he got to the spotlight was when he rose at the celebrations in London and toasted the team, adding that he was 'one of the proudest men in the room'.

He went on to disclose some details of their preparations:

'That morning they had a nice, quiet talk at which their plans were devised and what gave him special satisfaction was that every player had attempted to play as they planned. Every player gave of his best and was prepared to take the advice of an old, experienced player.'

The closest he got to a comment was a reported conversation with his old friend 'Olympian' of *The Buff* who wrote:

'There could be no mistaking the joy of the Blackburn Rovers party when they met at the Hotel Russell after the match to celebrate their victory and not the least pleased was Bob Crompton who has this season given many hours of his time to supervising the Rovers players. To him is due no small share of the credit for the achievement of the team. But when I had a few moments conversation with him he was much more sedate than were some of his colleagues.

'What I am pleased about most is that the Rovers have demonstrated beyond all doubt that they can play football with the best. Some critics have gone out of their way to say that we are not a good team and that we have been lucky. Today they have got their answer.'

It was not until the AGM in March 1929 that Crompton received a tribute from the board of directors, chairman Walsh offering his thanks 'for the creditable results that attend his supervision over and interest in the players'. Crompton, it was reported, replied that 'he had no desire to take much credit himself for the little extra work involved'.

Nationally there was a feeling that the FA Cup triumph was belated compensation for Crompton's publicised failure to win a medal, but 'Olympian' did not form the opinion that he connected the two. His judgement concurs with all local comment. The lack of a cup medal was behind him and could never be compensated. Management was not a substitute for playing.

Within days of the return to Blackburn the club embarked on a tour of Vienna, Budapest and Prague. The party consisted of 14 players, the secretary and trainer and nine of the ten directors, led by chairman Walsh. Left behind to hold the fort and attend the league meeting at which the fixtures were set was Crompton. A pragmatist who never believed he should avoid the mundane work at the club, he was spotted the following year acting as a steward when a huge cup tie at Ewood, between Rovers and Bolton, threatened to be ruined by the sheer volume of spectators. A Bolton fan spotted him and called out, 'Now then, cut it out. I'll fetch McEwen to you.' The Bolton press interpreted the jocular remark as referring to the difficulty Crompton used to experience in facing the Bolton player, but many were aware that it might also have its roots in the broken jaw suffered in the charity match in Belfast. Crompton took the ribbing with a smile. He was already planning how to take the team to another level. In the following seasons the club finished seventh and then sixth. It was the kind of steady improvement that Crompton anticipated and 1930/31 promised little difference.

On Monday, 16 February, completely out of the blue came the news that the management of the club was under scrutiny. On the Saturday Rovers went out of the FA Cup in dismal fashion at Chelsea, but it turned out that no one inside the club was surprised. During the week, 16 of the senior players had presented a petition to chairman Walsh, detailing a string of grievances against Crompton. Walsh had passed the round robin to Crompton who immediately stood down from any contact with the team, or indeed the club. The only explanation of the unrest was that the players were unhappy with Crompton's belief that the game was evolving, and more speed was needed, combined with accurate passing to maximise ball retention. It was obvious that Rovers' players were ageing and clearly feeling the pressures of Crompton's desire to improve their speed.

The affair could have been ended immediately by a few words from the chairman, but this was not forthcoming. *The Buff* pointed out that 'the board should have been aware of any unpleasantness and grasped the nettle themselves'. Crompton had little choice but to take the action he did and, given the fact that he had always acted without remuneration, his restraint in keeping the matter private was remarkable. It could be argued that Rovers' training was not going to suffer under the veteran trainer Moy Atherton, but that raises a question. Did the board of directors believe that Crompton had no impact as a manager or was it a convenient method of ridding themselves of a 'troublesome priest'?

A round robin is totally alien to the normal conduct of a club dressing room. Even in clubs where the manager has 'lost the dressing room', revolt is never so organised. Few are the clubs without a strong character who would voice a complaint. The Rovers team contained Jock Hutton, Herbert Jones, Bill Imrie, Jack Roscamp, Bill Rankin, Jack Bruton, Sid Puddefoot, Harry Healless, Jack Bruton and Arthur Cunliffe. Ten experienced players and hardly a shrinking violet among them. Yet the majority must have signed the complaint. It is hard to believe that Hutton or Rankin would not have sought direct confrontation. If that was the case and Crompton had ignored them a transfer request would have arisen. Crompton was clearly mystified at the grievances so clearly no confrontations had arisen. Later all but one or two of the players admitted that they regretted their actions. Examining the evidence, it is hard to believe that the action was instigated by the players themselves and one must wonder whether it had been orchestrated by a hand who sought to find a greater voice at the AGM.

Speaking in 1959, Billy Hough, who played for Rovers under Crompton in 1938/39, explained how he viewed the manager:

'I had particular respect for Bob Crompton who was the team manager. He had the Rovers in his blood and never stopped telling us how proud we should be to wear the blue and white. He could be a martinet, but you knew where you stood with him and everything he did was fair and without malice. He had a code and he insisted you complied with it.'

Unrest among the shareholders and the directors who represented them had been simmering. Some shareholders believed that the blame for the postwar malaise at the club lay with the directors, and there is little doubt that they had a fair case. There were those who thought they had solutions to the problems but lacked the platform since they could not gain sufficient votes to be elected to the board. In January 1927 they forced an extraordinary meeting at which two resolutions were to be put to the vote. The first was that the club's AGM should be moved from June to March. The reasoning behind this was that the club's annual retained list should be decided by directors who would be in situ for most of the following season.

The second was a more complex one regarding the voting on the election of directors. At each general meeting five directors, selected in rotation, had to retire. They could seek re-election, against other candidates who received the required nomination. Votes cast were weighted according to a shareholders' holding. The problem that had been arising was that some shareholders were not voting for five candidates but naming only a lower number of candidates and the club had been treating such votes as null and void, on the grounds that it stated that the vote was for five directors. This was believed to have the effect of allowing the directors to perpetuate their positions.

The rebels won the first vote, and it was agreed that the accounting date of the club would be changed to the end of February with an AGM in March, but they lost the second vote by 137 to 86. Alderman George Burke, a cotton manufacturer and town councillor, appeared to be the rebel spokesman, and he proposed an amendment to the motion that led to a heated dispute with chairman Walsh that took in points of procedure and ended with Burke refusing to acknowledge an order from the chair to resume his seat. A shareholder, T.P. Campbell, who had been a first-class referee, warned that cliques were forming in all directions. His warnings were prophetic.

The failure of the club to progress was the ostensible excuse for rebel shareholders to express their discontent but, when the next meeting was held in March 1928, the team was clearly improving. It placed the rebels in a quandary. Complaint would lack credibility, but something was needed to maintain the momentum of their campaign. They elected to launch an attack on the results obtained by the reserves. The necessity to reply was handed to Crompton. Furiously he rounded on the critics. He agreed that the reserve team was not all that could be desired but stated that some of the shareholders did not seem to appreciate the difficulties. He pointed out that, anxious to bring out their own talent, they had been introducing young players who instead of being helped by members of the club were being discouraged. He then added, 'You have apprentices in your own trades, and you don't expect them to do a man's work. You do not give the local players a chance. It is disgraceful sometimes to hear the language that is used. I have it from the players that they prefer to play away from home. I hope a little more charity will be shown in future.'

Typically, Crompton had answered with the honesty that marked his conduct. Whether or not he was aware, or cared, that his response lacked political astuteness is impossible to evaluate. His candour brought him dangerous enemies and he appeared unconcerned that to keep his place at the club he needed support when his turn came for re-election. A more conciliatory tone might have smoothed the situation, but Crompton only saw one road, the straight one. Additionally, his position was not helped by the fact that one of the youngsters he was trying to protect was his own son, Wilfred.

Successful conspiracies rely on timing, and it is relevant that the round robin affair surfaced in February, a month before the AGM at which Crompton was due to retire and had put himself forward for re-election. The press had disclosed little of the unrest in deference to the club's interests, but Crompton found that he had no option but to present the facts so that the shareholders did not vote under misapprehensions:

'I feel, as one who has served the Rovers for 34 years, and being now in business, that my position needs to be stated in order to remove misapprehensions. I was amazed when the chairman showed me the round robin of the 16 players in the first instance, for I had not an inkling that there was any dis-satisfaction among the playing staff. I have "fathered" some who have signed, have never bullied any, and what instructions have been necessary have been given quietly and privately in what I think were the best interests of the club.'

He disclosed that following the Chelsea tie the board sanctioned the chairman and Crompton to interview the players to seek to bridge the differences:

'That interview did not take place until last Thursday morning [5 March] and there were present the chairman and nearly all the players who signed the round robin. I invited each player to state his grievances and in more than one case there was none at all. I have been accused of being an autocrat but when I put this to the players not one of them substantiated it. In one or two instances there was clear evidence of misunderstanding and, taken altogether, the complaints proved, in my opinion, to be of quite a trivial character. There was nothing to justify the writing of the round robin. I gathered that more than one player regretted having signed it. I must say that when the chairman showed it me in the first instance, I was amazed, for I had not an inkling that there was any dissatisfaction among the playing staff. I have taken a great interest in some of the young players who signed the document and my experience and ideas have been given with the sole intention of benefitting them and the club. My views of playing tactics never differed from those we employed when we won the cup. Further, my instructions to any individual players have always been given privately and quietly.'

The time delay before the interviews took place heightens the belief that vested interests were pulling the strings. With players, manager and chairman available daily a gap of over a fortnight in a matter so pressing is inexplicable. The relative success of the club under Crompton had turned the tide for those in power, the directors. The reform movement had lost ground from the moment Crompton stepped in since they could no longer point to an underperforming club. That did not stop ambitions and a plot against Crompton a month before the AGM at which he sought re-election would only be to the benefit of the rebels. The lack of defence offered by the directors and their delay of proceedings hints that the board's strategy was to sacrifice Crompton, an action which under the voting system would profit the remainder of the retiring directors. Just before the vote, George Burke withdrew his nomination, a tactical move to wrong-foot the opposition.

Even so the voting at the annual general meeting at the Lecture Hall, Northgate, on 19 March 1931 shocked the town.

J.W. Walsh	1,626
T. Holden	1,402
W. Tempest	1,396
F. Wood	1,262
E. Jenkins	1,208
J.W. Rayton	1,052
J. Caton	1,035
R. Crompton	852
J. Cotton	844
J. Eddleston	659
P. Neild	633
J. Cotton junior	409
E. Porter	182

The reformers had achieved their biggest triumph since the agitation commenced. In addition to Crompton, Richard Birtwistle's son-in-law John Eddleston and the heir of the Cotton dynasty, John Cotton, lost their seats. Walsh and Walter Tempest had sufficient allies among the major shareholders to be in no serious danger but the sight of

Blackburn's greatest son coming eighth in the voting was simply unimaginable.

Crompton was perhaps his own worst enemy. Never a man to suffer from paranoia or megalomania, he simply ignored or was unaware of such dealings. This facilitated him becoming embroiled into the affair. As a latter-day Ewood manager, Tony Parkes, wryly observed, players are motivated by little more than self-interest in their preferences. He had reason to be cynical since his 34 years' service (this appears to be a fateful number) with Rovers was terminated by actions which indicate similar dark forces at work. Parkes joined the club in 1970. At the time he was a centre-forward who had scored goals at Buxton but found it difficult to attune to the pace of higher-grade football. On the training field he was a different proposition, a player with surprising control who was hard to dispossess. Ken Furphy reasoned that he was naturally a midfield player and successive managers, Gordon Lee, Jim Smith and Howard Kendall, were grateful for that decision. A badly broken leg terminated his career but while trying to rehabilitate he was asked to coach the youth and reserve sides. A new manager, Bobby Saxton, appointed him first-team coach and when he was dismissed five years later Parkes had his first spell as caretaker. It was the start of a spell in which he held a variety of roles and often acted as caretaker manager, his success in this capacity making him a football notoriety.

When Jack Walker took over Rovers, he was an owner who was close to the players. For tax reasons he lived in Jersey and his time in the UK had to be limited. However, he bought Jersey Airlines so that he could get in an out without the necessity of an overnight stay. Any businessman who was as successful as Walker has his methods of keeping his finger on the pulse and he developed a respect for the judgement of Parkes, who perfectly fitted the profile Walker was looking for. Although a Sheffield man, Parkes had entered the life of the town so that he was regarded as a local, an achievement in a town as insular as Blackburn. He had moved into a house behind the Horden Rake, up Livesey Branch Road, not ideal for a football professional. Raucous Friday nights would often see Parkes sleeping with his head under the pillow to catch some sleep before Saturday's game. The Rovers of his time was a small-town club. In recent years the players commute from Cheshire and probably few have seen the town centre but, in the 1970s, it was common to meet players like Parkes, Derek Fazackerley and Ken Beamish strolling around the shops and exchanging banter with the fans. The trio were also in great demand at fundraising events and seldom disappointed. Walker, Blackburn through and through, appreciated these qualities but it was Parkes's lack of self-interest that made him unique. Walker found that if he wanted an honest, unprejudiced account, there was no better source. Within the inner circle of the club, it was known that he used Parkes as his eyes and ears, and he always affirmed that Parkes would always remain at the club in some capacity.

Unofficial arrangements have the capacity to create problems, but Parkes never wore his ambassadorial role on his sleeve. Nevertheless, envy is never far from the surface in a football club and there were those, both players and management, who resented the arrangement. Some dealt with the situation pragmatically. Graeme Souness, perhaps the manager who appreciated Walker the most, made Parkes his assistant manager and even after Walker's death it was assumed that Parkes would always be on the staff. It came as a shock to everybody in 2004 that, when Mark Hughes had become the manager, Parkes was dismissed. It was a particular shock to Parkes who found out about his dismissal from his daughter, who had heard it on the radio. The subsequent citing of an administrative blunder and empty apologies lacked sincerity and the offer of a testimonial smacked of hypocrisy. No organisation whose core business is dealing with personalities with inflated and fragile egos could be so administratively inept as to leak the news of a man's dismissal before they informed him. If this judgement appears too harsh one needs only to ask one question: 'Would this have happened if Jack Walker had been alive?' Parkes was as much a victim as Crompton and for not dissimilar reasons.

Crompton, like Parkes, knew better than to publicly disclose his thoughts:

'I must thank all the people who have voted for me. My 34 years' experience with the Rovers has been a nice time and I have enjoyed every year I have been connected with the club. One is not a little disappointed at the result. It is all in the game, however. One has to take it as it is given. I thank you all.'

Crompton's absence from Ewood caused him to miss his son Wilf's last two appearances for Rovers. Although Wilf was kept on the books for a further season he was then released and joined Burnley. Bob still had plenty to keep him active looking after his business interests, but football had not completely been obliterated from his curriculum and at the end of February 1932 he applied for the manager's position at Manchester United. Clearly his recent history did him no favours because in June the club appointed Scott

Duncan, although because the role was secretary-manager it may be that Duncan's administrative background gained him the post. In his first season he narrowly avoided getting United relegated to the Third Division and, although he later got them promoted, he also was still manager when they were relegated to the Second Division.

When Peter McWilliam left Middlesbrough in March 1934, Crompton was linked with the vacancy. He denied that he had been involved in discussions with the directors but there was a growing feeling that he had too good a football brain to remain absent from the sport. At the start of 1935, Jim Ward of the Blackburn Unemployed Group asked him if he would spare them the odd hour to talk about the 'principles and finer arts' of the game. Never a man to disappoint, he agreed but went further, turning up to watch them play and often giving half-time advice, although he never attempted to have any say in the running of the team. Crompton recovered a taste for the game and when sounded out by Bournemouth in the close-season he indicated his interest. Negotiations were protracted, partly because Crompton was out of communication. Sam McClure had introduced him to sailing when they had first met, and Crompton had got a taste for the sport. He bought a yacht which he kept on the Wyre and spent his summer vacations on the sea. It was not until the middle of June that the news came that he had accepted the offer and would take over the Third Division team in the last week of July. Apparently severing his ties with Rovers, he sold his house and business interests and embarked on southern life.

His engagement was something of a coup for the Dorset club and by the turn of the year gates had doubled. It was a strange experience for Crompton in a league where he knew none of the players and where he did not even inherit a team, having lost many players when their contracts expired in the summer. Not that expectations were high since the team had finished 15th, 18th, 21st and 17th in the past four seasons. By the time that he arrived on the south coast, the directors had proceeded as always and signed replacement players. Of the players he inherited, only one could be described as outstanding, wing-half George Farrow, who signed for Blackpool a year later. He had a passable left-wing in the experienced Billy Chalmers and Eddie Parris, who was a one-cap wonder with Wales. Bournemouth had also signed a reasonable goalscorer, Joe Riley from Bristol City, although proof of the directors' hit-and-miss record was that they also signed Meynell Burgin from Tranmere. The scorer of 21 goals in 31 games on Merseyside, he never settled and played only four games under Crompton.

Crompton could see that the team lacked leadership with the loss of the veteran centre-half Alf Messer. This forced him to make his only signing, the Indian-born George Bellis, who had played for Wrexham, Wolves and Burnley. Displaying the ability to adapt to the circumstances he maintained the team in a position to challenge for promotion. On New Year's Day he was spotted in Blackburn, and it was anticipated that he would watch Rovers play Derby, his first visit to the ground on a matchday since the round robin. Instead, he was guest of honour at Darwen. Undoubtedly the neighbouring club enjoyed the situation and few Rovers fans did not interpret it as a deliberate slight to the club. Crompton, as ever, remained inscrutable and the *Blackburn Times* attempted to lower tension by pointing out that he might well have been scouting the form of the highly rated Darwen players, Harry Rawcliffe and Harry Jackson, as well as the Lancaster left-winger, Clark. It was further pointed out that Bobbie Aitkenhead, son of Crompton's old colleague Wattie Aitkenhead, had just broken into the Darwen team. Crompton professed to be enjoying life in management and living on the south coast and appeared to be a man who had made a clean break with the past. A month later came the news that he had resigned his position due to disagreement with the directors on footballing policies.

Despite the ease he had displayed in adjusting in the south he immediately returned north, although not to Blackburn. The dream of many working-class Blackburnians was to spend their retirement on the coast at Blackpool and several of the most successful achieved it. Despite his great fame, Crompton had not set his sights higher, and he obtained a residence in Holmfield Road. In the quieter North Shore area, it was the first street inland from the coast and ran parallel with the promenade. With a walk of 100 yards, Crompton would have been standing on the sand and more importantly breathing the sea air. Great importance was given to the medicinal benefits of sea air at the time, but it must have been additionally sweet to one raised in the perpetual smoke of the Blackburn mills.

Back at Ewood the club had commenced a long decline. Crucially Rovers sought no experienced ex-professional player to replace Crompton but promoted Arthur Barritt from the post of secretary to manager. He had no experience of looking after playing affairs, but his appointment handed the directors the control they had lost to Crompton. Every fan believes he can run a football club, and the directors were merely fans who through their financial means had reached the point where they could almost indulge their dreams. Without Crompton the board were free to acquire or sell players and above all select the team. Of course, having to reach consensus among themselves was always a problem but they no longer had an obdurate Crompton undermining their decisions. The organisation had been bequeathed a solid core from Crompton's years but far too quickly the side deteriorated. A goalkeeper at the time, Bill Gormlie, later observed, 'We were poorly trained at Ewood, six laps round the pitch or that sort of thing. We were left to our own resources.' A lack of support was crucial. Barritt declared, 'Gates would hardly keep a Lancashire Combination Club going.'

A series of decisions upset the fans. Long-serving trainer Moy Atherton was dismissed without explanation. Then Arthur Cunliffe and Ronnie Dix were sold to Aston Villa. This prompted the vice-chairman, W.H. Grimshaw, to resign. The annual general meeting only intensified the acrimony. Chairman J. W. Walsh was likened to Mussolini over his handling of the Atherton dismissal. Alderman Grimshaw, who had not initially detailed his reasons for resigning, did so: 'I left them because I could see no salvation if that was going to be the policy of the Rovers directorate, to sell players instead of trying to get one or two cheap or otherwise to help the club.'

Arthur Tempest took issue with Grimshaw, and a slanging match ensued in which Tempest alleged that Grimshaw had told him, 'Everybody thinks that we as directors ought to find a lot of money, but I am one who is not digging in my pocket. If any team comes for any player, they can take him if the price is right.' Grimshaw denied this. There were seven seats up for election to the board.

Seventh in the poll came Walsh, who commented, 'It is a vote of no confidence in the chairman.' The following day he resigned after 21 years as a director. Barritt had a hopeless task in trying to steady the ship. In March 1936, with relegation inevitable, Barritt resigned.

The board's response was risible. They assumed official control of the playing staff and appointed Reg Taylor as secretary to deal with the administration. By October, the team was failing to cope with life in the Second Division and the board had to admit that they were incapable of managing the playing side. Taylor was appointed as secretary-manager, a move almost identical to the strategy with Barritt that had so signally failed. While respected as an administrator and a man who was known to have an eye for a player, he had no experience of handling professional players and like Barritt became increasingly out of his depth. In March 1938, relegation to the Third Division appeared probable and in town there was a clamour for the return of Crompton.

Rumours spread and the fact that negotiations had taken place were disclosed in the *Northern Daily Telegraph*:

'At the meeting last night [29 March] Blackburn Rovers' directors unanimously endorsed the suggestion of the secretary-manager [Mr Taylor] that, in view of the Rovers' position, Mr R. Crompton should be asked to give what assistance he can to the club. Mr Crompton has agreed to do so and until the end of the season will co-operate with Mr Taylor in the management of the team. From now onwards Mr Taylor and Mr Crompton will jointly have full control of the team and will suggest its composition for the approval of the board of directors. Mr Crompton has consented to render all the help he can in the circumstances and his services, which will begin immediately, will be in a purely honorary capacity in the interests of the club itself.'

In fact, the press release was compiled by Harry Kay of the *NDT*, who was asked to compose a diplomatic statement which would announce Crompton's return, without giving the impression that anyone had gone cap in hand, or that anyone had done any climbing down, or had weakened on matters of principle, or had done anything contrary to conviction.

No one has ever disclosed whether Taylor really made this suggestion, although it would appear to be a strange idea for a man who had the role of manager. However, this prevented the directorate from an admission that they had been forced to beg for Crompton's return. Crompton's acceptance of the press release appears to have been magnanimous, although subsequent events indicate that he was playing a long game. Rovers were 18th when Crompton returned to Ewood, promising nothing in the way of improved results. Nine matches remained and after averaging a point a game relegation was avoided. Behind the scenes, Crompton played his cards and on 25 May the news came that he would be taken on as the manager of the team on a remunerated basis.

'He will have full control of the players and training and as at the end of the past season will co-operate with R.H. Taylor in matters affecting the club,' it was reported.

Life for Crompton must have been as sweet as at any time in his long association with Rovers, but he was not a man to absorb himself in self-congratulation. Like the fans he was hurt to see the club outside the top flight and he endeavoured to change matters.

*Bob Crompton,
Blackburn Rovers
captain, in 1903/04*

The Blackburn
Rovers team of
1903/04. Back
row, left to right: A.
Bowman, R. Evans,
N. Walton (trainer),
J. McDonald, S.
McClure. Middle: A.
Whittaker, G. Smith,
R. Crompton, A.
Monks, F. Blackburn.
Front: J. Dewhurst,
W. Bradshaw.

John Cameron and
Bob Crompton,
Blackburn's
outstanding full-backs
in 1904/05.

Blackburn Rovers squad of 1905/06. Back row, left to right: George Smith, MacGill, Jock Cameron, Bob Evans, Billy McIver. Middle row: R.B. Middleton (secretary), Sam Wolstenholme, Joe Wilson, Bob Crompton, Jimmy Robertson, Jack Birchall, Fred Pentland, R Holmes (trainer). Front row: Jimmy Moir, Arnold Whittaker, Billy Bradshaw, Billy Davies, Adam Bowman, Miles Chadwick, Sam McClure.

THE BLACKBURN TIMES, SATURDAY, APRIL 6, 1907

A Famous Blackburn Football Team.

The football team, a portrait group of whom is given herewith, was well known in Blackburn long before the Blackburn Rovers came into being. It was known as the Brookhouse Football Club, and the players were mostly employed at Brookhouse Mill, and were captained by Mr. A. N. Hornby, then quite a young man, but as good a sportsman as ever walked. The club owed its origin to him. It played matches all over Lancashire. The code was Association, but of a type very different from that now played, and in some things closely approximating to Rugby. The team shown in the above group, reading from left to right, consisted of William Hill, blacksmith at the mill; William Graham, tackler; William Leeming, weaver; A. N. Hornby (captain); Stephen Fawcett, secretary of the club, now residing at Sunny Bank, Wilpshire; Ralph Duxbury, spinner, deceased; W. Little ("Red 'un"), spinner, deceased; John Parren, drawer-in; Thurston Hesketh, foreman; Henry Cottam, warehouseman; and John Eastham, weaver, deceased. The team wore blue guernseys, blue caps, and white trousers. Others who played with them and against them pretty often were Joseph Law, now a bookseller in London; John Pickering, and John Deynes, an elder brother of Mr. Fred Baynes, of Samlesbury Hall. Mr. A. N. Hornby loved nothing better than to get up a team to play his own club, and very often he played in the opposing team, when the Brookhouse lot loved nothing better than to lay out their captain — a feat, however, it was difficult to accomplish. Mr. Hornby was also very fond of promoting sports in Brookhouse Fields, and great amusement was caused by women's races for new bonnets, etc.

Newspaper article from The Blackburn Times, *1907*

Bob Crompton in 1910. He made 530 appearances for the club and scored 14 goals.

British Championship, 1 April 1911, England 1 Scotland 1 at Goodison Park. Rival captains Bob Crompton, England, left, and Scotland's James Hay shake hands before the match as the referee William Nunnerley of Wales looks on.

British Championship at Goodison Park, 1 April 1911, England goalkeeper 'Tim' Williamson leaps to punch clear assisted by the England captain Bob Crompton.

Tottenham Hotspur v Blackburn Rovers. Captains Bob Crompton of Blackburn Rovers (left) and Bobby Steel of Spurs toss the coin before the game in 1911.

*Captain of England for the Home
International Championship match
against Ireland at Ayresome Park.*

International players from the four Home Nations in 1913. Left to right: Michael 'Mickey' Hamill (Ireland; Manchester United), Robert 'Bob' Crompton (England; Blackburn Rovers), Billy Meredith (Wales; Manchester United), and James Campbell (Scotland).

Blackburn Rovers in 1913/14. Back row left to right: Robert 'Bob' Holmes (trainer), Daniel H. 'Danny' Shea, John 'Jock' Simpson, George Chapman, Alfred Robinson, Percy James Smith, Albert Walmsley, Thomas Byrom. Front row: Edwin 'Eddie' Latheron, Arthur Cowell, Bob Crompton, William 'Billy' Bradshaw, Joseph C. 'Joe' Hodkinson.

Bob Crompton (seated front, right) with the championship-winning squad of 1913/14.

Blackburn undertook two major continental tours before the First World War. Pictured here before one of those games overseas.

Displaying the FA Cup in 1928 before the start of the season opener against Portsmouth, which they won 6-0. Director Bob Crompton is back row, second left.

Throughout his spell as honorary manager, protocol dictated that management decisions came from the board of directors, of which Crompton was a member. The buying and selling of players and even team selection was theoretically the subject of a collective decision. Even though it was apparent that Crompton had some autonomy in decision-making, the sensibilities of the directors precluded this becoming common knowledge.

This changed the moment that Crompton's position became a remunerated one. In the close-season he started to rebuild the team. He spent what little money he had on the Aston Villa half-back George Hardy, who was earmarked to lead the team. The other three players were an ageing centre-forward, Jack Weddle from Portsmouth, and young men in Billy Rogers from Preston and 'Nobby' Clarke from Birmingham. Perhaps even Crompton had no idea what the masterplan was, but he was determined to introduce speed into the attack. Although he commenced with two trusted veterans, Jack Bruton and Billy Guest, on the wings he was not long in noting their lack of rapidity and he turned to Rogers and a youngster from Burscough Victoria, who played in the Mid-Week League, Bobby Langton. Clarke was an immediate success, a natural goal poacher who combined well with the veteran Weddle. Ideally Crompton would have preferred a younger man, but Weddle was a scientific trainer and a good influence on and off the field.

Crompton noted early in the campaign, that apart from the experienced Len Butt, there was a lack of artistry, so he turned to a man who had plenty of class but was on the transfer list because he was considered too frail for league football, Arnold Whiteside. The two combined quickly but their lack of physical presence tilted the balance of the side and Crompton conceded he had been mistaken with Hardy and moved big Bob Pryde from left-half to the centre-half position. He had recognised that Frank Chivers, an average inside-forward, had the hard-working, fear-nothing qualities that might be better used at half-back and introduced him in Pryde's stead. The goalkeeping had oscillated between the mercurial and agile Gerry Matier and the less gifted Jimmy Barron. Matier was capable of a brilliance that Barron could never match but he was showy and made mistakes. At Carrow Road he once threw himself full length to catch a spectator's cap that had been caught by the wind. Crompton opted for the steady, consistent man.

After the tinkering of the first weeks of the season, the team gelled. Clarke struck his 20th goal in the middle of January and promotion was always a probability. To prove that they had quality they beat Swansea, Southend and Sunderland in the FA Cup before losing to Huddersfield when they were realistically dreaming of a Wembley appearance. The Sunderland tie went to three games, which did not help with fixture congestion, but the team had character. Fresh from the disappointment of their cup exit they had a crucial game against Coventry, who had won at Ewood Park earlier in the season. A single, spectacular goal from Butt won the game for Rovers and permitted them to embark on an uneventful close to the season which saw them promoted as champions. On a personal basis it was proof that Crompton was not just a great player but a fine manager.

The question that remains unanswered is just how talented a manager Crompton was. He had in truth been a remunerated manager for only one season and a half (six months with Bournemouth and the 1938/39 season with

Rovers) but his achievements were impressive. He had maintained Bournemouth in the top six throughout his spell in charge and had Rovers promoted as champions in his only season. It was not a record to compare with Herbert Chapman, but it was one that could scarcely have been bettered. At both clubs he had taken over a team who required rebuilding and had to do so with virtually no transfer funds available. He was adept at spotting weaknesses and improving players and had a clear idea of style and approach. Unafraid to replace fading veterans with younger players, he was never afraid to admit a mistake or act accordingly. Fitness and speed were key facets of his style and he ensured that these were improved. In the 1928 FA Cup Final he had decisively won the coaching war. On the negative side the evidence is undeniable that he found some players notably unreceptive to his suggestions. Whether with resources and opportunity he would have joined the great names of management is unproven. The fact is that with little in his favour he was remarkable successful.

Jack Weddle, who remained in the game long after he retired, detailed the philosophy that Crompton brought to the club:

'The success of Blackburn Rovers last season can be laid down to the adoption of attack as the first policy. It was part of our game policy to throw all our weight into attack and roughly speaking to leave the defence to do their own work.'

This time, because Crompton was a paid employee, the press could pay appropriate tributes, the *Blackburn Times* writing:

'Tribute has already been paid in this paper to the influence of Mr Robert Crompton whose recall to the club has been justified to an extent even greater that his most ardent admirers had a right to expect. He has been the brains and hands which has moulded the team with its spirit, confidence and method.'

An earlier tribute in the *Times* had read, 'He has used his wide powers of team selection wisely and his playing of a settled side has been one of the chief factors in the club's recovery and in the "happy family" spirit that existed among the team.'

All of this makes the 'round robin' incident that ended Crompton's first spell of management even more perplexing.

Even the directors gave Crompton his dues, although the words of the chairman John Cotton are open to interpretation. At the annual general meeting when commending Crompton, Len Evans, the trainer, and Mr Meek, the masseur, he stated, 'He thought he [Crompton] would be the first to admit that he has been allowed to manage.'

There was wide anticipation in the town following the promotion but Crompton while remaining confident and optimistic was blunt, 'We have no money to spend so it's no use expecting stars.' His ability was not put to the test. Life was overshadowed by the gathering clouds of war and after just three games the 1939/40 Football League season was abandoned. After a hiatus of two months, the regionalised War League was formed, and the team was more or less kept together. In the only national competition, the War Cup, Rovers reached the final at Wembley. With Evans and the coaches, Ted Harper and Jack Bruton, unavailable because of immediate call-up, keeping the club running became the responsibility of Crompton and Reg Taylor. Soon Crompton bowed out of Ewood for the final time. The responsibility for the team became essentially an administrative one with guest players roped in to cover enforced service absence. Taylor, the club secretary, was an obvious choice for this role since he had experience and was known throughout the football world. With the country on a war footing, it made no sense from him to commute from Blackpool.

7

The story ends

THE DIVORCE from Blackburn was not complete and from time to time Bob Crompton slipped back to watch Rovers and renew acquaintances. On 15 March 1941 he found the attractions of the derby against Burnley impossible to resist. He appeared to enjoy the afternoon, welcomed back by many old friends and watching one of the men he helped improve at the club, Len Butt, score two goals in a 3-2 win.

After saying his farewells, he went to take tea with friends William Barton and his wife in their home in Eldon Street, just off Shear Brow. After the meal he complained of feeling unwell and, while resting in the sitting room, collapsed and died. He had been receiving treatment for a heart condition for some months.

It was inferred that the visit to watch Rovers was an isolated one but there is evidence to the contrary. On the evening of 18 January 1941 Crompton's car was in collision with a van delivering parcels at the junction of East Park Road and Brantfell Road. A youth in the van, Fred Hyde of St Jude's Road, was taken to hospital with two broken legs.

The accident occurred close to the home of the Bartons and it appears probable that he was calling in on them after having watched Rovers at Bury.

The austerity of wartime and the problems of winter travel curtailed the extensiveness of the funeral arrangements and the attendance of many of his friends and acquaintances. It was held in St John's Church on the Thursday following his death. In keeping with Crompton's wishes, the service conducted by the vicar, the Rev. Edgar Bell, was a simple one, with only the size of the congregation denoting that one of the town's greatest men had reached the end of his life.

Inevitably the public's attention focused on the old players in the congregation. Travel difficulties limited these to men who lived in Blackburn. Two men who were at the club when Crompton first signed, Harry Chippendale and James Stuart, were the oldest. There were also the veterans of the championship teams: Alf Robinson, Tommy Suttie and Wattie Aitkenhead. Walter Crook, who was Rovers' captain at the time, was there as representative of the team. The only non-Blackburn player to appear was Tom Bamford, the old Burnley full-back.

Also present were the widows of Eddie Latheron and Harry Garstang, plus Harold Readett, who had been taken on by Crompton as a junior player in 1928, Harry Aspden Watson, an insurance agent and descendant of a Scottish draper, James Watson who opened up the insurance company in Richmond Terrace, Arthur Albert Tattersall, an Accrington man who manufactured emery wheels, Lawson Duxbury, a Revidge cotton manufacturer, Charlie Milford, a Leeds man who had played amateur cricket for years and was the secretary of East Lancashire

CC, Fred Hargreaves, the secretary of the Lancashire FA, Robert Blackshaw who had been licensee of the Cemetery Arms, William Edward Bracewell of Burnley, a member of the Lancashire FA and FA, John William Duckworth of the Blackburn District Combination, Arthur Victor Sagar of the Blackburn Thursday League, G.H. Smith of Kidderminster, M. Parker, a member of the old Blackburn Trinity club, Councillor Fred Shaw and Christopher Hindle of the Wholesale Fruit Merchants' Association, J. Yates JP, Harry N. Patterson, the editor of the *Blackburn Times*, Harry L. Kay and F.G. Marton of the *Northern Daily Telegraph*, R. Wilkinson, H. Cooper, Syd Smith, Albert V. Bannister (managing director of a printworks), A. Longworth, F. Pearce of Kinder Brothers, A. Whalley of Whalley Brothers, H. Walmsley, J.R. Peel, the market superintendent, G. Swindlehurst, J.H. Robinson, Watkin I'Anson (son of the old Blackburn town clerk and original Rovers shareholder), R. Charnley of Loxhams, S. Berry, R. Munroe, James Crank and J.S. Crank (local builders), J.H. Fielding, T. Marsden, Mr and Mrs G.D. Yates, Sam Isherwood (his old mechanic), Mrs E. Woolfall, Mr and Mrs F. Hindle, Mr and Mrs A. Ainsworth, J.W. Atkinson, T. Byrne, R. Ormerod and John Sweeting (ex-manager of Thwaites Brewery then retired and licensee of the Dog Inn).

The directors turned out in force led by the chairman John Cotton and his deputy Fred Wood. There was also Tom Blackshaw, N. Culshaw, Arthur Duckett, George Norman Forbes (nephew of Johnny Forbes), W. Kenyon and Walter Tempest, who was the serving mayor. Accompanying them were the secretary Reg Taylor, and the club's solicitor Robert Ferguson.

The local dignitaries present were Aldermen J. Aspin and R. Culshaw, ex-Alderman W. Kenyon, and councillors J.J. Pickering and J. Shorrock.

Members of the Harwood family of Darwen who were linked with the Cromptons through marriage attended, namely Councillor J. Harwood, Mrs H. Harwood, Miss D. Harwood and Miss E. Harwood. The funeral arrangements were carried out by another family member, Harry Harwood.

At all funerals of great individuals, the congregation contain those representing official bodies or connected through the contacts of working life. There are also those family and close friends who were classified as the mourning party. In the case of Crompton these were his wife Alice, his son Robert and Robert's wife Ethel, his daughter Alice Haworth, and his youngest son Wilfred along with his wife Isabella. The other family members were Robert and James, sons of his brother Robert, and his wife's sister Maude Pomfret and her husband, Albert. The remainder were personal friends William Barton and his wife, in whose home Crompton had died, and his long-time business partner 'Tinker' Davies. The final couple were Ernest and Clara Brindle. Brindle came from Audley and had been a reserve half-back with Rovers between 1903 and 1905. His career had been modest but the disparity in their achievements had not hindered his friendship with the great man.

Perhaps nothing is more demonstrative of Crompton's withdrawn nature than the size of the list of his personal friends. Crompton was never a man for idle socialising or cheap popularity. Conversely, he was not a man who was anonymous in the town and there were many who could relate stories of when they met the great man. Of course, the premium tales were from those who knew him before he was famous. George William Ridsdale, a woodwork teacher at the technical college, was able to dine out for years on stories of how, when working on the house of Sir John Rutherford, he used to play during his dinner hour in scratch games with a strapping young player who looked 'quite useful'.

Crompton did get an 11-line obituary in *The Times*. It was tucked under the account of the game between the British and the Allied Armies. The final word goes deservedly to a man who played under Crompton, Walter Crook, who became a well-known trainer. When questioned about his methods he replied concisely, 'What was good enough for Bob Crompton is still good enough for me.'

Appendix one

Crompton's penalty record

Date	Opponents	Venue	Goalkeeper	Competition	Result of kick
16/01/1904	Nelson	H	Walker	Lancs Cup	Scored
27/02/1904	Manchester United	A	Sutcliffe	Lancs Cup	Scored
19/03/1904	Notts County	A	Pennington	League	Saved
23/04/1904	Liverpool	H	Platt	League	Scored
19/11/1904	Notts County	A	Earle	League	Scored
11/03/1905	Manchester City	A	Hillam	League	Scored
01/04/1905	Newcastle United	H	Lawrence	League	Scored
18/09/1905	Manchester United	H	Montgomery	Lancs Cup	Saved
09/10/1905	Darwen	H	Lill	ELCC	Scored
02/04/1906	Bolton Wanderers	H	Davies	League	Saved
05/11/1906	Bolton Wanderers	Clayton	Broomfield	Lancs Cup	Missed
04/01/1908	Aston Villa	A	George	League	Scored rebound
18/01/1908	Middlesbrough	A	Williamson	League	Missed
14/11/1908	Manchester United	H	Moger	League	Scored
01/01/1909	Preston North End	H	McBride	League	Saved
15/04/1911	Newcastle United	A	Lawrence	League	Scored
13/03/1915	Everton	H	Fern	League	Scored
03/04/1915	Burnley	A	Dawson	League	Scored
10/04/1915	Tottenham Hotspur	H	Jacques	League	Scored

Goals from free kicks

Date	Opponents	Goalkeeper	Comp
02/01/1897	Notts County	Toone	League
02/09/1899	Manchester City	Williams	League
08/04/1907	Everton	Sloan	League
23/01/1915	Manchester United	Beall	League

Own goals

Date	Opponents	Goalkeeper	Comp
15/10/1898	Sunderland	H	League
24/04/1899	Burnley	H	ELCC
23/02/1901	Stoke City	H	League
29/12/1901	Liverpool	A	League
18/01/1902	Sheffield United	A	League
29/03/1902	Notts County	H	League
08/10/1904	Sunderland	A	League
19/11/1904	Notts County	A	League
31/12/1904	Bury	H	League
21/11/1908	Everton	A	League
12/12/1908	Notts County	A	League
02/12/1911	Manchester City	A	League
30/12/1911	Bury	A	League
19/10/1912	Liverpool	A	League
20/12/1913	Manchester United	A	League
27/12/1913	Liverpool	A	League

Appendix two

The footballing friends of Bob Crompton

SAMUEL McCLURE
Defender
Born: Harrington, 11 February 1877
Died: Workington 17 July 1906
Debut: 23 September 1899
Final game: 28 April 1906
First goal: 12 January 1901
Final goal: 21 October 1905
Career: St Michael's School; Black Diamonds; Everton;
Workington; Blackburn Rovers

The most charismatic of players, McClure was an extraordinary sportsman who could achieve anything. He played sport from infancy and became a great sailor, rower and swimmer and competed in professional athletics as a sprinter. In his hometown he became legendary for playing football in the morning, rugby in the afternoon and football at night, all in organised games. However, he was almost lost to the game because of work. After working locally as a reporter for the *Free Press* and *The Sun* he obtained a position as sub-editor on the *Evening Echo*, in Dublin. Within three hours of setting foot on Irish soil he reported on the Ireland-Scotland international. In May 1895 the paper folded, and McClure returned to Workington, working as a labourer before being made manager of Mrs Suart's printing and stationery business.

By September he was keeping goal for the Black Diamonds where he won six medals in various competitions in Cumberland and played in every position. It was as a goalkeeper that he made his impact, being signed by Everton, but inaction was not to the liking of the big man and he returned to play for Workington. Rovers spotted him when they signed his team-mate Swift. McClure quickly showed the club that he could play anywhere but his debut was scheduled as a goalkeeper. A late injury to centre-half Bob Haworth prompted a switch, McClure played in defence, the deputy goalkeeper did well, and it was McClure who went back to the reserves. He started to see more action as a defender and even when selected in goal could not always be prevented from switching with a colleague if he was not seeing enough action.

First-team chances started coming his way, at half-back and the club found they had a real treasure, a genuine hardman who never shirked a tackle, ran all day, and refused to take a backward step to anyone. At his best the England selectors considered him, but his style was not deemed subtle enough. An ever-smiling giant without an enemy in the game he had the company of his brother, curiously nicknamed 'South African', for a spell and married the sister of Bob Crompton's wife but it was his friendship with Bob Haworth that most remembered. The pair spent much time sailing and sometimes took along team-mates, although few ever volunteered for a second voyage with this intrepid pair.

He was to die young, only two years after he was married, mourned even more in the town that had come to love him than his hometown. He had survived one illness in which he lost much weight but recovered until an abscess in his ear spread inwards.

After a service in Workington, he was buried in Blackburn, and he never saw his son play in the Harry Boyle Cup Final or his brother Alex become a professional with Birmingham. A second-generation Irishman, his parents John and Eliza came over to the Whitehaven area but eventually settled in Workington where John was a bricklayer. Sam always maintained his home in Workington and in Blackburn used to lodge with the Hodsons on Audley Range, Hannah Hodson being a native of Workington.

Football League: 144 appearances, 12 goals
FA Cup: 8 appearances
Total: 152 appearances, 12 goals
Lancashire Cup: 14 appearances

WILLIAM 'TINKER' DAVIES
Centre-forward
Born: Wrexham, 13 April 1882
Died: Preston 21 January 1966
Debut: 2 September 1905
Final game: 27 April 1912
First goal: 9 September 1905
Final goal: 21 October 1911

Career: Wrexham National School; Wrexham St Giles; Wrexham Victoria; Wrexham; Blackburn Rovers; Grangetown

Wales: 9 appearances 5 goals

Honours: Football League championship, Welsh Cup x 2

At the age of 17 Davies became the sole support of a family of seven. The 14s 6d per week he earned in an engineering works was insufficient and so he took to the roads selling pots and pans, which earned him his nickname. Fearless and ruthless on the football field he launched his small frame and terrorised goalkeepers with his shoulder charges. He scored strikers' goals, nipping into dangerous areas close to goal, but also goals for the connoisseur where he ran from deep beating man after man. Once asked to repeat a startling goal for the benefit of the new movie camera, he obliged until walking the ball into the net he trod on the ball and fell. A businessman from an early age, he was for 20 years a partner to Bob Crompton. In March 1917 he returned on leave from service with the Mechanical Transport Corps in Malta to marry Edith Cotton, the niece of the Rovers chairman, having already commenced work in the family cotton business.

Football League: 132 appearances, 66 goals

FA Cup: 11 appearances, 3 goals

Total: 143 appearances, 69 goals

Lancashire Cup: 17 appearances, 19 goals

War League: 1 appearance

ERNEST 'LUMBER' BRINDLE
Left-half
Born: Blackburn, 15 July 1885
Died: Blackpool, 4 November 1942
Debut: 9 January 1904
Final game: 25 January 1904
Career: St Silas's; Park Villa; Audley Range; Blackburn Rovers; Accrington Stanley; Chorley; Great Harwood; St Matthew's

The son of Isaac Brindle, a weaver from Audley, he trained as a blacksmith. Brindle and his half-back partner James Shuttleworth were signed on amateur terms by Rovers in July 1903 after playing in the Blackburn Amateur League for Audley Range. He had also helped St Silas's to the championship of the Blackburn Amateur League and played for Park Villa. He was rated highly with the reserves but played in only two Lancashire Cup ties, against Nelson and Everton. He signed for Accrington in 1905 and had many years with them, having a benefit game against Rovers in August 1910. He signed for Chorley in August 1912 before joining Great Harwood in 1913. Just before the war he was playing for St Matthew's. He died at his home in Newton Drive, Blackpool, at the age of 57.

Lancashire Cup: 2 appearances
War League: 1 appearance

Appendix three

Obituary by John K. Fletcher, *Bolton Evening News*

'Crompton was a magnificent specimen of manhood. He had the physique which fitted him to cope with the most vigorous opponents though he rarely made the fullest use of his weight, preferring to rely upon his footballing abilities to carry him through. It was his policy to play the ball rather than the man and yet at one period he fell foul of some referees for offences in the penalty area not all of them merited, much to his suspicion and distress for he was a particularly honest and sportsmanlike player. He was however inclined to put on weight and that required him to train all the year round, cricket claiming his attention in the summer and he was also a cyclist and later took up motoring.'

Appendix four

Contemporary water polo players

JOHN ATKINSON
Born: Blackburn, 8 February 1881
Died: Blackburn, 9 December 1945

Atkinson became a master tailor and had outfitters shop in Penny Lane for 43 years. In 1924 he was elected as a councillor for the St Stephen's ward and served for 21 years. He was made an alderman in 1933. A member of the swimming club, he played in the forward line of the polo team from 1892 but moved to half-back in 1895. He had elite-swimmer speed but lagged behind men like the Kay brothers, George Brown, and Harry Ward. It was said in his obituary that he was capped by Lancashire.

JAMES BELL
Born: Blackburn, 9 December 1880
Died: Blackburn, December quarter 1957

A joiner, he was a committee man of the swimming club and was reserve goalkeeper behind Joe Kay junior.

GEORGE BROWN

Born: Blackburn, 24 May 1873

Died: Blackburn, 14 August 1948

Brown was the son of James Brown, a bricklayer from Stockport, and Maria (nee Forrest). The couple married on 28 September 1854 and settled in the Witton area before

George was born in Chapel Street. In addition to Chapel Street, the family lived in Belgrave Street, Cowell Street and Hancock Street. Brown was spotted in local galas by Joe Kay, who eventually persuaded him to join the swimming club in 1892. He took time to make his mark but in 1895 he started to finish prominently in the races, although beaten in the major events by Harry Ward and Bob Crompton. He started to appear in the water polo team, his ability to play in any position except goal, making him an invaluable member of the team.

Brown appeared in the Lancashire trials in 1902 and

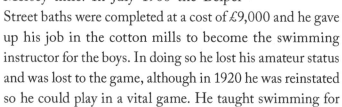

1903 and on 25 August 1904 turned out on the right wing for Lancashire against the Western Counties. Blackburn players had appeared in the county trial previously, but he was the first to gain county honours. During the year he came sixth in the Mersey mile. In July 1906 the Belper Street baths were completed at a cost of £9,000 and he gave up his job in the cotton mills to become the swimming instructor for the boys. In doing so he lost his amateur status and was lost to the game, although in 1920 he was reinstated so he could play in a vital game. He taught swimming for four years before he took the licence of the Prince of Wales in King Street, where he remained for 22 years. For the first five of them he was chairman of the water polo club.

He married Esther Elizabeth Pickup on 26 October 1899 and their sons Jack (born 1900) and George (born 1907) became players for the town's water polo team. Jack was the most proficient and on 2 September 1922 he played for England against Ireland. George became a publican, taking over the Prince of Wales in King Street. On retirement in 1934 he went to live in Nook Terrace, Cherry Tree, but on the death of his wife in 1948 he went to live with his daughter, Ada Brindle, in Palatine Road. He died there three months later in a house next door but one to his son George.

FRANK JONES
Born: Blackburn, 18 July 1878
Died: Blackburn, March quarter 1969
Jones was the son of Francis Lloyd Jones who founded the Jones Brothers organisation that supplied the Blackburn mills. Frank managed the heald and reed arm of their repertoire. The family lived in Audley Place though Frank eventually moved to Wyldham, near Beardwood.

JOSEPH GOLDEN KAY
Born: Blackburn, 21 November 1862
Died: Heywood, 25 November 1944
Kay was the son of Henry and Elizabeth Kay who were drapers in Bond Street. He became a hairdresser with a shop in Fielden Street. He helped form the first Blackburn Swimming Club in 1879 and was an active racer and water polo player. In all he spent 14 seasons with the water polo

team, four of them as captain. In June 1900 he was employed by the corporation as swimming instructor at the Freckleton Street baths and could no longer compete. During his long spell in this job, he never missed a day through illness, was instrumental in teaching more than 20,000 children to swim and helped train an English champion in Tom Morris, three Lancashire champions and 11 North-East Lancashire champions. For over 50 years he never missed an annual general meeting of the swimming club. His son Joe played water polo for Blackburn after the war. In the early days  water polo was embryonic with goals being the full width of the baths, either end, and no limitations on physical contact or underwater swimming. It was Kay who guided the water polo team through the period when rules evolved.

RILEY KAY

Born: Blackburn, 25 February 1870

Died: Blackburn, 20 June 1953

Seven years younger than his illustrious brother Joe, Riley was arguably a better swimmer. He won the captain's race three times where Joe never did but was probably not as proficient a water polo player as his brother. When Joe started work at Freckleton Street baths in 1900, Riley took over his hairdressers in Fielden Street. Later between the wars he took over his brother Thomas's tobacconists. His son Henry moved to New Bedford, Massachusetts, where he became a champion open-water swimmer. In 1908 he beat the American champion Carl Michelsen by 100 yards, over five miles of the Acushnet River. The American declined the offer of a rematch.

JOHN MORGAN

Born: Kendal, March quarter 1855

Morgan was the son of an Irish couple, James (an umbrella maker) and Jane Morgan, and was brought up in lodgings in Kendal. He married a woman from Pennsylvania, Mary Jane Dennison, but the marriage did not appear to last. He moved to Blackburn and lived in Cooper Street, where he worked as a shoemaker with his children, but by 1901 he was back in Kendal, in lodgings. He was a noted swimmer and won the captain's race at the swimming club eight times. He also played with the water polo team in the early days of 1892 and 1893. There was always a suspicion that he was not the kind of man the club liked to have as captain and the annual race was contested with some vigour by establishment figures like Joe and Riley Kay and George Brown. In 1887 the Kays sunk to a low in sportsmanship when Joe deliberately dropped two lengths in arrears so that he could pace his brother. Happily, the tactic proved unsuccessful, and Morgan won by two feet. In December 1892 Morgan was in court, fined 20s for fighting in Nook Lane and a further shilling for an unspecified offence in his cell.

JACOB REDFERN

Born: Accrington, March quarter 1879

Died: Blackburn, June quarter 1917

Although Redfern was born in Accrington he was brought to Blackburn when he was still a toddler. The family – he was the eighth of nine children – lived in Warwick Street and then Hodson Street. His father Richard was a stonemason and Jake followed him into the occupation although both subsequently moved into different fields. Richard became the licensee of the Black Horse in Northgate. Jake became mate on the *Maggie*, a barge operating around Widnes. Around 1896 Jake started turning out for the squadron team at the swimming club. His speed was such that he was given a trial in the forward line for the water polo team, at a time when Bob Crompton was the star player. In 1901 he attempted to beat the club record (held by Finney at four and half minutes) for staying under water. He managed three minutes.

JAMES ROBERTSON
Born: Preston, 1872
Died: Blackburn, December quarter 1911
The son of George Robertson, who had a coach building business. The family lived in Bond Street, just round the corner from the Redfern house.

HENRY WARD
Born: Blackburn, 18 April 1871
Died: Blackburn, 16 January 1958
The son of John Ward, a brush maker from Butler Street, Henry followed him into the family business, branching

out to incorporate barrel making. He joined the swimming club and was good enough to win the captain's race at his first attempt in 1894. He went on to win it a further three times. Henry started playing centre-forward for the polo team in 1895. Between the wars he became a full-time swimming instructor and moved to live in St Alban's Place, which is where he died at the age of 86.

Appendix five

Family tree
- Ellis Crompton: born Darwen, 1755; buried Darwen, 28 February 1826; married Mary Bradshaw, 9 April 1787, Blackburn

Children
- John: baptised Darwen, 19 February 1788; buried Darwen, 30 April 1788
- John: baptised Darwen, 6 March 1789; married Betty Harwood, 2 February 1818, Blackburn
- Edmund: baptised Darwen, 27 June 1791
- Ellis: baptised Darwen, 6 January 1794; died Darwen, 6 July 1830
- Martha: baptised Darwen, 21 July 1796; married William Jepson, 8 March 1922, Blackburn
- James: baptised Darwen, 14 December 1799; died Darwen, 1848; married Nancy Ainsworth, 3 January 1819

Children of James Crompton and Nancy Ainsworth
- Sarah: born Darwen, 1820; died Darwen, December quarter 1884; married William Baron Watson, 12 April 1846, Blackburn
- Elias: baptised Darwen, 16 September 1821; died Darwen, September 1869; married Betty Jackson, 28 March 1842, Blackburn

- Mary: baptised Darwen, 16 March 1823
- Betsy: baptised Darwen, 27 March 1825; died Darwen, March quarter 1895; married Walmsley Bury, 2 January 1843, Blackburn
- Thomas: baptised Darwen, 24 October 1828; married Margaret Harwood, 1 January 1847, Blackburn
- Jane (Jenny): baptised Darwen, 24 October 1828
- James: born Darwen, 18 March 1831; died Darwen, December quarter 1911; married Esther Heyes, 16 June 1853, Darwen
- Crompton: born Darwen, 1832; died Farington, June quarter 1918; married Mary Ellen Morris, September quarter 1856, Darwen
- Ainsworth: born Darwen, 1842; died Darwen, September quarter 1853
- Joseph: born Darwen, 1842; died Blackburn, September quarter 1917; married Ellen Feilden, December quarter 1865, Darwen
- Edward: born Darwen, 1844; died Blackburn, September quarter 1913; married Mary Harwood, June quarter 1867, Darwen
- Mary Jane: born Darwen, March quarter 1848; baptised Darwen, 31 May 1848

Children of Elias Crompton and Elizabeth (Betty) Jackson
- James: born Darwen, September quarter 1842
- Elizabeth: born Darwen, June quarter 1845
- Nancy: baptised Darwen, 22 December 1847; buried Darwen, 1 January 1848
- Robert: born Darwen, June quarter 1849; died Blackpool, 25 December 1914
- Thomas: born Darwen, December 1851; buried Blackburn, 19 June 1852

Children of Robert Crompton and Alice Utley
- James: born Blackburn, June quarter 1874; died Blackburn, March quarter 1928; married Margaret Ellen Kirkham, March quarter 1899, Blackburn
- Harry: born Blackburn, 18 March 1878; died Blackburn, 25 May 1891
- Robert: born Blackburn, 26 September 1879; died Blackburn, 15 March 1941; married Ada Ingham, July 1901, Blackburn
- Charles: born Blackburn, 23 March 1881; died Blackburn, 16 April 1898

Children of Robert Crompton and Ada Ingham
Harry: born Blackburn, 9 March 1902; died Blackburn, 29 September 1927

Robert Ingham: born Blackburn, 21 October 1902; died Blackpool, January 1986; married Ethel Smith, June quarter 1929, Blackburn

Thomas: born Blackburn, June quarter 1905; died Blackburn, 25 September 1905

Alice Ingham: born Blackburn, 13 January 1907; died Blackburn, June quarter 1944; married John Haworth, March quarter 1929, Blackburn

Wilfred: born Blackburn, 1 April 1908; died Lytham, 22 June 1971; married Isabella Wilding, June quarter 1934, Blackburn

Grandchildren of Bob Crompton
Children of Robert Ingham Crompton and Ethel Smith
Robert: born Blackburn, 10 August 1931
Helen: born Blackburn, September quarter 1933
Patricia: born Blackburn, September quarter 1938

Child of Wilfred Crompton and Isabella Wilding
Jean Teresa: born Blackburn, 27 July 1938; married Cyril
Terence Fenton, Blackburn, 15 January 1959

Children of Robert Ingham Crompton and Ethel Smith
Robert: born Blackburn, 10 August 1931
Helen: born Blackburn, September quarter 1933
Patricia: born Blackburn, September quarter 1938

Child of Wilfred Crompton and Isabella Wilding
Jean Teresa: born Blackburn, 27 July 1938; married Cyril
Terence Fenton, 15 January 1959, Blackburn
Robert, the last of the direct male Robert Crompton line,
had two girls
Lesley (born Blackpool September quarter 1958) and Lynn
(born Blackpool September quarter 1960).
He represented his grandfather when he was elected to the
Football League Museum Hall of Fame in 2018.

* Dates of births, deaths and marriages were not available
for every player listed in the appendix or the biography
sections. Other detail such as dates of baptisms and burials
has been added to give as complete a picture as possible.

Appendix six

Crompton's greatest ever selection
Sam Hardy (Liverpool, Aston Villa, Nottingham Forest)
Dickie Downs (Barnsley, Everton)
Herbert Burgess (Glossop North End, Manchester City, Manchester United)
Ben Warren (Derby County)
Billy Wedlock (Bristol City)
Peter McWilliams (Newcastle United)
Jock Simpson (Blackburn Rovers)
Jimmy McMenemy (Celtic)
Jimmy Quinn (Celtic)
Eddie Latheron (Blackburn Rovers)
Albert Smith (Burnley, Bradford Park Avenue)

Appendix seven

Blackburn Rovers Captains

	From - To	Pos	Birthplace	Age
Thomas Greenwood	1875	GK	Blackburn	19
Fred Hargreaves	1878	WH	Blackburn	19
Jimmy Brown	1883	CF	Blackburn	21
Jimmy Forrest	1886	WH	Blackburn	22
Herbie Arthur	1887	GK	Blackburn	24
Johnny Forbes	August 1888 – October 1893	FB	Bonhill	26
Geordie Anderson	October 1893 – August 1897	HB	Edinburgh	22
Tom Booth	August 1997 – May 1898	HB	Denton	23
Geordie Anderson	August 1998 – March 1899	HB	Edinburgh	26
Tom Booth	March 1899 – May 1900	HB	Denton	24
Bob Crompton	August 1900 – August 1905	RB	Blackburn	20
Bob Evans	August 1905 – May 1906	GK	Wrexham	24
Bob Crompton	August 1906 – May 1915	RB	Blackburn	26
Percy Smith	August 1919 – May 1920	CH	Corby	38
Levy Thorpe	August 1920- March 1922	HB	Seaham Harbour	30
David Rollo	March 1922 -May 1924	RB	Belfast	30
Harry Healless	August 1924- August 1932	HB	Blackburn	31
Bill Imrie	August 1932 – March 1934	HB	Methil	24
Jack Bruton	March 1934 – November 1935	RW	Westhoughton	30
Bob Pryde	November 1935 – August 1936	HB	Methil	22
Charles Calladine	August 1936 – March 1938	WH	Wessington	25
Len Butt	March 1938 – May 1938	IF	Wilmslow	27
Walter Crook	August 1938 – May 1939	LB	Whittle le Woods	25
Bob Pryde	August 1946 – May 1949	CH	Methil	33
Dennis Westcott	August 1949 – February 1950	CF	Wallasey	32
Eric Bell	February 1950 – August 1951	LH	Bedlington	28
Bill Eckersley	August 1951 – May 1956	LB	Southport	26
Bill Smith	August 1956 – September 1956	U	East Stonehouse	29
Ronnie Clayton	September 1956 – May 1969	RH	Preston	22
Ken Knighton	August 1969 – March 1971	MF	Darton	25
Allan Hunter	March 1971 – September 1971	CB	Sion Mills	24
Terry Garbett	September 1971 – September 1972	MF	Lanchester	26
John McNamee	September 1972 – March 1973	CH	Coatbridge	31
Mick Heaton – team captain	August 1973 – Jun 1974	RB	Sheffield	26
Roger Jones – club captain		GK	Upton on Severn	27
Graham Hawkins	August 1974 – October 1977	CB	Darlaston	32
Tony Parkes	October 1977 -August 1979	MF	Sheffield	28
Howard Kendall	August 1979 – May 1981	MF	Ryton	33
Derek Fazackerley	August 1981 – May 1986	CB	Preston	29
Glenn Keeley	August 1986 – May 1987	CB	Ilford	32
Nicky Reid	August 1987 – May 1990	MF	Davyhulme	26
Kevin Moran	August 1990 – May 1993	CB	Dublin	34
Tim Sherwood	August 1993 - February 1999	MF	Borehamwood	24
Jason Wilcox	February 1999 – May 1999	LW	Bolton	28
Lee Carsley	August 1999 – August 2000	MF	Birmingham	24
Garry Flitcroft	August 2000 - September 2003	MF	Turton	26
Barry Ferguson	September 2003 - January 2005	MF	Hamilton	25
Andy Todd	January 2005 – August 2006	CB	Derby	30
Lucas Neill	August 2006 – January 2007	RB	Sydney	28
Ryan Nelsen	January 2007 - November 2011	CB	Christchurch	29
Chris Samba	November 2011 – January 2012	CB	Créteil	27
David Dunn	January 2012 – May 2012	MF	Great Harwood	32
Danny Murphy	August 2012 – March 2013	MF	Chester	35
Scott Dann	March 2013 – January 2014	CB	Liverpool	25
Grant Hanley	January 2014 -May 2016	CB	Dumfries	23
Jason Lowe	August 2016 - May 2017	MF	Billinge	24
Charlie Mulgrew	August 2017 - May 2019	CB	Glasgow	31
Elliott Bennett	August 2019 – May 2021	MF	Telford	30
Darragh Lenihan	August 2021 – May 2022	CB	Dunboyne	26
Lewis Travis	August 2022	MF	Whiston	24

Appendix eight

Blackburn Rovers' players who played right back for their country

Doc Greenwood	England
Tom Brandon	Scotland
Bob Crompton	England
David Rollo	Ireland
Jock Hutton	Scotland
Keith Newton	England
Henning Berg	Norway
Jeff Kenna	Republic of Ireland
Lucas Neill	Australia
Brett Emerton	Australia
Adam Henley	Wales
Ryan Nyambe	Namibia

Blackburn Rovers penalties conceded

	No.	Foul	Handball	Games	Ave/gm
Glenn Keeley	20.5	14.5	6	412+6	20
Bob Crompton	20	15	5	576	29
Arthur Cowell	14	9	5	307	22
Derek Fazackerley	12.5	10.5	2	671+3	54
Colin Hendry	10	9	1	399+9	40
Matt Woods	9.5	4.5	5	307	32
Bill Eckersley	9	6	3	432	48
Willie Kelly	9	4	5	202	22
Herbert Jones	8	3	5	262	33
Keith Newton	8	5	3	357	45
Lucas Neill	8	6	2	225+4	28
Tom Wylie	7	4	3	191	27
Darragh Lenihan	7	6	1	218+15	31

Blackburn Rovers own goals

	No	Games	Ave/gm
Bob Crompton	15	576	38
Matt Woods	9	307	34
Colin Hendry	6	399 + 9	66
Herbert Jones	4	262	65
David Gray	4	107	27
Alf Robinson	3	157	52
Shane Duffy	3	69 + 1	23

Index